PRESSURE GROUPS, POLITICS AND DEMOCRACY IN BRITAIN

CONTEMPORARY POLITICAL STUDIES SERIES

Series Editor: John Benyon, *Director, Centre for the Study of Public Order, University of Leicester*

A series which provides authoritative yet concise introductory accounts of key topics in contemporary political studies.

Other titles in the series include:

UK Political Parties since 1945
Edited by ANTHONY SELDON, *Institute of Contemporary British History*

Politics and Policy Making in Northern Ireland
MICHAEL CONNOLLY, *University of Ulster*

Local Government and Politics in Britain
JOHN KINGDOM, *Sheffield Polytechnic*

British Political Ideologies
ROBERT LEACH, *Leeds Polytechnic*

British Government: The Central Executive Territory
PETER MADGWICK, *Professor Emeritus, Oxford Polytechnic*

Race and Politics in Britain
SHAMIT SAGGAR, *Queen Mary and Westfield College, University of London*

Selecting the Party Leader
MALCOLM PUNNETT, *University of Strathclyde*

Does Parliament Matter?
PHILIP NORTON, *University of Hull*

The President of the United States
DAVID MERVIN, *University of Warwick*

The Politics of Economic Policy
WYN GRANT, *University of Warwick*

Introduction to International Politics
DEREK HEATER, *formerly of Brighton University* and
G.R. BERRIDGE, *University of Leicester*

Elections and Voting Behaviour in Britain (2nd Edition)
DAVID DENVER, *Lancaster University*

The Law and Politics of the British Constitution
PETER MADGWICK and DIANA WOODHOUSE, *Oxford Brookes University*

PRESSURE GROUPS, POLITICS AND DEMOCRACY IN BRITAIN

Second Edition

WYN GRANT

Professor of Politics, University of Warwick

HARVESTER
WHEATSHEAF

New York London Toronto Sydney Tokyo Singapore

First published 1995 by
Harvester Wheatsheaf
Campus 400, Maylands Avenue
Hemel Hempstead
Hertfordshire, HP2 7EZ
A division of
Simon & Schuster International Group

Typeset in 10/12pt Times
by Dorwyn Ltd, Rowlands Castle, Hants.
Printed and bound in Great Britain by
Biddles Ltd, Guildford and King's Lynn

Library of Congress Cataloging in Publication Data

Grant, Wyn.
    Pressure groups, politics and democracy in Britain / Wyn Grant. —
2nd ed.
      p. cm. — (Contemporary political studies series)
    Includes bibliographical references and index.
    ISBN 0 7450 1672 3
    1. Pressure groups—Great Britain. 2. Lobbying—Great Britain.
3. Great Britain. Parliament. House of Commons. I. Title.
II. Series.
JN329.P7G73 1995
322.4'3'0941—dc20   94–30434
                                               CIP

British Library Cataloguing in Publication Data

A catalogue record for this book is available from
the British Library

ISBN 0 7450 16723 (pbk)

1 2 3 4 5 99 98 97 96 95

CONTENTS

Preface   vii

I INTRODUCTION: THE KEY CHARACTERISTICS OF
       PRESSURE GROUPS   I
       What is a pressure group?   3
       Social movements   5
       Political parties   8
       A working definition of a pressure group   9
       Typologies of groups   13
       A classification of group strategies   15
       Pressure groups and democracy   23

2 PRESSURE GROUPS AND THE POLITICAL SYSTEM   27
       Pluralism   28
       Policy networks and policy communities   34
       Corporatism: yesterday's theory?   37
       The liberal critique of pressure groups   39

3 HOW PRESSURE GROUPS INFLUENCE WHITEHALL
       AND THE POLITICAL AGENDA   47
       Getting issues on the political agenda   49
       Food additives: a case study of issue emergence   51
       Influencing the executive branch of government   57
       Policy implementation and enforcement   63

4   PARLIAMENT   66
Ways of using Parliament   67
Professional lobbyists   74
Conclusions   78

5   EXERTING PRESSURE OUTSIDE WHITEHALL
**   AND WESTMINSTER**   80
Pressure groups and the party system   80
Pressure groups and the media   84
Pressure groups and the courts   89
Local government   91

6   PRESSURE GROUPS AND THE EUROPEAN UNION   98
The decline of the national route?   100
European-level pressure groups   104
The targets of representation   110
The leading role of big business   114
European corporatism?   121

7   THE EFFECTIVENESS OF PRESSURE GROUPS   125
Why measuring pressure-group influence is difficult   127
A typology of factors affecting pressure-group effectiveness   130
Conclusions   149

8   CONCLUSIONS: PRESSURE GROUPS AND DEMOCRACY 153
The legacy of Thatcherism   155
Labour in office?   157
The case for pressure groups reviewed   159
The limits to pressure-group power   164

References   166

Index   177

Preface

This book seeks to provide a general introduction to the role of pressure groups in British democracy for those relatively unfamiliar with the subject. Readers who wish to follow up the subject in more depth by reading some of the academic literature on pressure groups can refer to the list of references at the end of the book.

Since the first edition of this book was published, a considerable amount of important new work has been undertaken on pressure groups in Britain. Of particular significance has been the British Interest Groups Project at Aberdeen University coordinated by Grant Jordan and his colleagues (referred to hereafter in this book as 'the Aberdeen group'), and the work on lobbying at the European Union level undertaken by Sonia Mazey of Cambridge University and Jeremy Richardson at Warwick University.

As well as making use of what is now an extensive literature on pressure groups, this book draws on interviews I have conducted over the years with pressure-group officials, politicians and civil servants. Some of this research has been funded by the Economic and Social Research Council and by the Nuffield Foundation.

I would like to express my appreciation to the series editor, John Benyon, for originally suggesting that I should write this book. The second edition was prepared while I was a Visitor at Nuffield College, Oxford. I would like to thank the Warden and Fellows of Nuffield College for inviting me to be a Visitor, and particularly

my sponsor, Vincent Wright. While I was there I had the opportunity of meeting Mancur Olson again. I do not agree with all his
views, but I have always found his work stimulating. Not all academics who have accomplished so much are as open or approach-
able, or as willing to discuss their work with anyone, whatever their
standing.

This book is dedicated to the memory of my uncle, Sidney Field,
who sadly died before publication of the first edition. Conversa-
tions I heard as a child in his newsagent's shop in Plumstead, SE18
helped to stimulate my interest in politics, and gave me my first
lessons in looking for the story behind the story in the day's
newspapers.

I would like to thank Sophia Grant for her help with materials
on the Motor Cycle Action Group. As always, special thanks are
due to my wife, Maggie, who was writing up her own work on
pressure groups at the same time as I was working on this second
edition.

Wyn Grant
Oxford, June 1994

1

Introduction: the key characteristics of pressure groups

Every four years or so the majority of British electors go to schools, village halls, and a variety of other polling stations throughout the country to cast their votes in a general election. In between the four-year intervals, a minority of voters exercise their right to vote in local and European elections. For most electors, voting is their main point of contact with the democratic process. Only a small and declining minority are members of political parties. More people are members of the Royal Society for the Protection of Birds (RSPB) than of the Labour Party. The majority of the electorate are, however, increasingly disengaged from the political process and, indeed, cynical about its workings and the likelihood of securing change. Even among the middle-class section of the population, only a minority are politically active. On a weekend, a typical middle-class person might visit a shopping mall and a garden centre; play tennis or squash; watch a video; enjoy a takeaway meal; and carry out minor repairs in the home. He or she is much less likely to engage in any form of political activity.

Every day, the paid officials and members of pressure groups are engaged in a wide variety of activities designed to influence the course of government policy. On a typical working day in London, there will be thousands of personal or telephone contacts between pressure-group officials and civil servants. For example, it is likely that officials from the Confederation of British Industry (CBI) will travel from their offices at Centre Point to meet civil servants at the Treasury or the offices of the Department of Trade and Industry (DTI) in Victoria Street. Officials of the National Farmers' Union will most likely be travelling across the capital from their headquarters to a meeting at the Ministry of Agriculture, Fisheries and Food (MAFF) just off Whitehall. In the lift, they might meet officials from the Food and Drink Federation who have made the short journey from their headquarters near Aldwych. Some of these contacts will be concerned with European Union (EU) proposals, and in Brussels, equally, officials of the European organisations representing a variety of interests will be travelling to the Commission's Berlaymont building or to its other offices scattered round the city.

Although many of the meetings will be between pressure-group officials and their counterparts in the civil service, many other types of contact will also be taking place. A junior minister at the Department of Health may be meeting a delegation of junior hospital doctors concerned about their working hours. In Parliament, lobbyists for the disabled may be shepherding a group of people with a particular disability towards a sympathetic group of MPs with whom to talk about the limitations of the provisions made by government to deal with their special needs.

Some of the activities taking place will be less orthodox in character, and are sometimes referred to as protest-group activities. The police may have to be called to a town hall when protesters opposing a proposed development get out of hand in the public gallery. Animal rights activists may be breaking into a research laboratory to rescue animals. Opponents of a new road may be lying down in front of bulldozers, or resisting attempts by the police and bailiffs to evict them from houses along the route.

Clearly, pressure-group activity represents an important part of the political process in Britain; certainly, more citizens are involved in pressure-group activity than in political parties. The period since the 1970s has seen a proliferation of 'cause' groups, particularly those concerned with environmental issues, ranging from global pollution problems to the protection of a particular species of animal. Groups representing 'sectional' interests, such as the British Medical Association or the Chemical Industries Association, continue to play a significant role in the political process. Business alone is represented by over 1,800 associations.

Much of this book will be concerned with explaining how pressure groups set about seeking to influence political decisions. How are they organised, and what kinds of strategies and tactics do they use? However, an attempt will also be made to tackle broader issues about the role of pressure groups in a democracy. Does the existence of such groups enhance the democratic process, or undermine it? Do the activities of pressure groups tend to reinforce existing distributions of power in society, or can they bring about fundamental changes? Before starting to answer these questions, it is necessary to explore what is meant by a 'pressure group'. A number of problems have to be resolved before a definition can be attempted.

What is a pressure group?

This book is concerned with groups that seek to influence public policy – which can be formulated by central government, local government, the European Union or, in some cases, by quasi-governmental organisations. The emphasis on public policy is important because any organised entity with the capacity to make authoritative decisions may develop internal pressure groups. For example, a firm may be viewed as a political organisation, and groups within it may lobby for a particular investment decision. In the case of a firm, such groups will not normally be formally constituted, but their identity will often be well known to other participants in a decision-making process. Other groups with decision-making authority may see the formation of advocacy groups with a particular purpose: for example, the successful movement for the ordination of women within the Church of England has been replicated by the formation of a like-minded but as yet smaller movement within the Roman Catholic Church. Another example was the group of members of the Cheltenham and Gloucester Building Society (C & G Alternatives) who sought to oppose its take-over by Lloyds Bank. Groups of this kind have their own fascination, but the focus of this book is on the political processes of society as a whole, rather than on particular organisations within it, however significant they may be either to their own members or to society in general.

This book is concerned with organised entities that have such characteristics as a defined membership, stated objectives in relation to public policy and, often, a paid staff working to attain those objectives. Focusing on such groups raises four difficult problems of exclusion through the use of a particular definition of a pressure group: the relationship between an 'interest' and the pressure groups that seek to promote that interest; the relationship between a 'social movement' and the pressure groups it generates; the problem of pressure exerted by a single actor such as a firm; and the problem of whether parts of the machinery of government itself can be regarded as pressure groups.

The first of these problems, then, is concerned with the relationship between an interest and the groups that represent that interest. 'Interest' is a word with many meanings. Some of these, such as a legal concern or pecuniary stake in property, or the payment of money to service a debt, obviously need not be discussed here. Other meanings, such as the idea of the selfish pursuit of one's own welfare, have value-laden overtones which are best avoided. The meaning of interest which is particularly relevant here is what the *Concise Oxford Dictionary* terms a 'thing in which one is concerned; principle in which a party is concerned; party having a common interest *(the brewing interest)*'. So defined, interest covers both the pursuit of causes (such as prison reform) and the promotion and defence of particular stakes in the economy (such as those of farmers).

However, interest has been especially used to apply to particular economic identities. Not all of these identities have been organised, at least not as a whole. For example, it has been common to speak of the 'City interest'. This has been considered a very influential interest in Britain for a long time. The influence of the City is often blamed for the overvaluation of sterling for long periods of modern British history, an overvaluation which damaged the international price-competitiveness of British manufacturing industry. However, the influence of the City did not rest on its possession of well-organised interest groups. The traditional channel for conveying City opinion to the government was through the Governor of the Bank of England. Very often, however, the influence of the City did not require any overt expression of view. Treasury officials and the City shared common, unquestioned assumptions about the need to maintain the value of sterling. Any sign of pressure on sterling as a result of a loss of confidence in the financial markets was often enough to persuade governments to change their economic policies.

Unorganised interests are, however, tending to diminish in significance. In the City, trade associations for various financial interests – formerly of little significance – have assumed a new importance. There is a variety of reasons for this particular change in the City, including a decline in its social cohesion, the removal of traditional barriers between different types of financial institution, a new regulatory regime which has transformed the role of many trade associations, and a greater openness in the relationship between the Treasury and the Bank of England. That is not to say that the Chancellor no longer sounds out City opinion at informal lunches, or that governments do not anxiously watch trends in market sentiment. Even so, the exercise of influence in modern conditions requires organisation. The study of pressure groups is the study of organised interests, although one must always be aware that behind well-defined organisations lurk more amorphous but nevertheless significant bodies of opinion.

Social movements

The discussion so far has focused on 'sectional' economic interests rather than causes, but problems can also arise in exploring the relationship between broad social movements and the pressure groups that spring from those movements. Consider one of the most important social movements of the late twentieth century: feminism. Women who consider themselves feminists hold a variety of views, and reflect those views in a variety of ways in their lifestyle. They would probably, however, agree that they are concerned with redefining the role, and reasserting the status, of women in a society which has previously been dominated by the assumptions and preferences of men. The required changes can be brought about in a number of ways. For many women, the most important change would be a mental one: thinking about the world in terms of feminist principles and arguments. This change of perception would affect the conduct of a woman's everyday life in terms of her relations with men and with other women; her relations with her family; and her career objectives and behaviour in the workplace. Many important changes can be sparked off by individual women reading feminist literature or watching television programmes with a feminist perspective, or discussing their reading and viewing informally with other women. It is possible for a woman to regard herself as part of the feminist movement without belonging to any organisation or even an informal mutual-help group.

Even so, it is clear that many of the goals of the feminist movement require political action if they are to be achieved. For example, better day-care facilities are necessary if women, particularly less well-off women, are not to be prevented from pursuing their careers. The feminist movement may have drawn attention to the serious problem of domestic violence, but political action is necessary to ensure that prolonged violence by a man can be claimed as a legitimate defence by a woman accused in the courts because she made a violent response to continued abuse, and funds are necessary to provide counselling, refuge and general assistance to battered wives. (For a discussion of women's aid, see Stedward 1987.)

Thus there is here a broad social movement of which pressure-group activity forms only one part. Indeed, women's aid groups have stressed such values as complete participation, the authenticity of personal experience, and collective self-organisation (Stedward 1987, p. 232). When pressure-group activity springs from a social movement, it may thus reflect the characteristics of that movement although, clearly, individuals subscribing to a broad goal – such as the abolition of hunting – may differ about how that goal should be achieved: a point to which we will return later in the book.

Another problem is the question of political pressure exerted by individual political actors, most importantly firms. It is clear that from the 1970s onwards in Britain there was a proliferation of direct political activity by firms, operating either through their own government relations divisions or through paid lobbyists acting on their behalf (see Grant 1993a). It would seem wrong to exclude this type of activity because it does not involve an organisation with a constitution, membership and paid officials. Jordan and Richardson (1987, pp. 14–18) are surely correct when they argue for a broad definition of pressure group that accepts companies and corporations as such groups. After all, such an approach meets the *Concise Oxford Dictionary*'s definition of a 'group' as a 'number of persons or things standing close together'.

But then, how wide does one cast the net? For example, should government ministries be treated as pressure groups? After all, the Ministry of Agriculture, Fisheries and Food has often been portrayed as the client of agricultural interests, whilst the Department of Trade and Industry has often been regarded as close to business interests. However, this could seem to be stretching the term too widely. Ministries do, of course, often fight for the departmental view within Whitehall, and that view often reflects to some extent the perspective and priorities of the pressure groups within the ministry's orbit, a phenomenon that will be explored more fully in Chapter 2 when policy communities are discussed. However, ministries always have to aggregate the views of their client groups, rather than simply acting as their representatives within the government machine. Aggregation often involves reconciling the divergent views of different groups; it will certainly involve placing their views within the context of both the policy of their own minister and that of the government as a whole.

Quasi-governmental organisations pose greater problems. Some of them have been set up in the past with one of their implicit functions being to act as a buffer between the government and particular pressure groups, e.g. the Countryside Commission, the Equal Opportunities Commission. Others have even been made responsible for mediating between rival groups, e.g. the Red Deer Commission which has sought to resolve conflicts of interest between sporting enthusiasts wishing to have a sufficient number of deer to shoot, and farmers annoyed at the damage done to their crops by marauding deer. The 'quangos' set up by the Conservative governments in the 1980s and 1990s have, however, been widely criticised for being filled largely with known government supporters who are then used to implement government policies without adequate democratic accountability. Such bodies may be particularly impervious to pressure-group activity.

Quasi-governmental organisations can act as pressure groups; they can belong to pressure groups; they can mediate between pressure groups, or between pressure groups and the government; but they may also be used as a mechanism to insulate policies against pressure-group activity. The range of their tasks draws attention to the fact that pressure groups function within a complex system of relationships which link a variety of political institutions and bodies. One sometimes has to look at pressure groups in isolation in order to understand their internal political and organisational dynamics, but one must also relate them to the broader political context in which they operate.

Political parties

Political parties belong to that broader political context. Pressure groups may exist within political parties, as, for example, the Socialist Educational Association or the Socialist Medical Association within the Labour Party, or the Conservative branch of the Campaign for Homosexual Equality. However, I would argue for a clear distinction between pressure groups and political parties. Political parties seek to win seats in elections either with the objective of forming the government or part of the government (the most usual objective) or to acquire sufficient seats to bring about or to prevent changes in the present constitutional arrangements of the country, a definition which could cover the Scottish and Welsh Nationalists and the various parties from Northern Ireland.

The range of concerns of political parties is typically wider than that of pressure groups. To be regarded as serious, they have to have policies which cover every conceivable issue of public interest, leaving aside those moral issues which are seen as a matter for personal judgement by individual MPs. The narrower concerns of pressure groups – with particular issues or interests – do not generally make contesting elections a viable strategy. Admittedly, they may do so to draw attention to the level of public concern on a particular issue (such as capital punishment) or to draw sufficient votes away from a particular party so as to make it lose a seat and think again about some aspects of its policies. In the 1991 Kincardineshire by-election, supporters of the Scottish regiments threatened by defence cuts discussed nominating their own candidate. In the event they did not, but:

> Even if this tactic had been pursued a realistic assessment would not have identified that grouping as a 'party'. It would have been seen as a pressure group adopting a particular tactic more generally associated with a party: it would not have *been* a party.
>
> (Jordan, Maloney and McLaughlin, 1992a, p. 3)

Pressure groups may, then, occasionally contest elections as a political tactic, although it is not a very effective one, and is mainly a sign of being outside the political mainstream. Sponsoring particular candidates selected by a political party, as some trade unions do in the Labour Party, is another matter, although again the political gains for the sponsoring body are questionable. In general, however, the distinction between a political party and a pressure group is a clear one. For example, at a number of points in the history of farmer representation in Britain, the possibility of organising a separate farmers' party has been discussed. The National Farmers' Union 'generally regarded a separate agricultural party as impracticable and over-ambitious – as indeed it was' (Self and Storing 1962, p. 44). Agrarian parties have flourished in Scandinavian countries with proportional representation, but have become part of larger groupings as the agrarian share of the electorate has declined, although some of the new democracies in Eastern Europe, such as Poland, have agrarian parties. Farmers in Britain decided to take the pressure-group route to pursue their interests.

A working definition of a pressure group

We have dealt with the problems surrounding the definition of a pressure group; it is now possible to offer a working definition:

> A pressure group is an organisation which seeks as one of its functions to influence the formulation and implementation of public policy, said public policy representing a set of authoritative decisions taken by the executive, the legislature and the judiciary, and by local government and the European Union.

This definition encompasses think-tanks such as the Institute of Economic Affairs (IEA) as pressure groups, even though they do not engage in what would conventionally be regarded as lobbying. They do, however, seek to change the intellectual climate of opinion, which in turn influences the policy agenda and options available to ministers. It is generally agreed, for example, that bodies such as the IEA played an important role in paving the way for Thatcherism, and that the Adam Smith Institute had an influence on the development of particular policies. Think-tanks are, however, a rather special type of pressure group which may have a close, if informal, relationship with a particular political party such as that between the Institute for Public Policy Research and the Labour Party. The influence of think-tanks within the Conservative Party has, however, declined under the Major Government: they had a special mission in the more ideological atmosphere of Thatcherism.

Primary groups and secondary groups

The basic definition may be elaborated by making a distinction between primary and secondary pressure groups. Relatively few pressure groups are concerned simply with the representation of the interests or views of their members, although many European-level groups offer little in the way of services. Most groups, however, offer services to members as a means of attracting and retaining their membership. In the case of an employers' organisation, this may be a sophisticated range of services from training courses and seminars at reduced prices for members, through advice on the effective use of information technology, to representation before industrial tribunals.

Groups pursuing particular causes usually provide their members with at least a magazine, and perhaps sell various goods to raise funds on which members are given a discount. In practice, of course, many different incentives to join are mixed up in membership appeals. The Aberdeen group give the example of a poster seen there, of which the printed portion said, 'Join UNA and help the UN put the world back together again'. A local addition said, 'Drink wine! Meet new people!' (Jordan, Maloney and McLaughlin, 1994a, p. 529). Opportunities exist to drink wine while meeting new people without joining a pressure group, but the Aberdeen group make an interesting case for a marketing perspective on pressure-group activities:

> Thus, the fact that the RSPB has 852,000 members while Plant Life has 1200 does not necessarily suggest that 'birds' are valued so much more by the population than plants, but that the pro-bird organisation has, over time, marketed itself much more successfully.
>
> (Jordan, Maloney and McLaughlin, 1994b, p. 549)

It may be, of course, that the population does have warmer feelings towards birds than plants, and that the RSPB has been very effective in mobilising those sentiments in an organisational

form. A distinction may be made, however, between those organisations where the service function either to members or to others
predominates, and those where services are provided as a membership incentive in order to recruit as large a portion as possible
of the eligible membership. In the first category are the seven
million or more members of the Automobile Association (AA)
who see its primary function as the provision of a breakdown
service, although the AA also lobbies government on transport
policy questions. Members are not particularly encouraged to at-
tend the annual general meeting (one can write in for details), and
the vast majority of them are concerned with its efficiency as a
service club relative to the other alternatives available (some of
them purely commercial). Should one be dissatisfied with the AA's
services, there are other providers of automobile rescue services
on the market. Individual members of the AA may not always
agree with its statements on transport policy issues, but are generally more concerned with its service function.

Similarly, the Cats Protection League exists primarily to provide
a rescue and rehabilitation service for abandoned and unwanted
cats, although it does undertake some lobbying on feline welfare
issues. Again, there are alternative providers of cat rescue services,
although some of these also rescue other animals. Some cat-lovers
may prefer to identify with an organisation that does not also
rescue dogs. In the case of animal rescue services, the rescued
animal does not, of course, have a choice about whether it is rescued and by whom.

The distinction between primary and secondary pressure
groups is not just one between the predominance of service provision compared with political representation in the organisation's work. There is a more general distinction between those
organisations whose primary purpose is political, and those
whose objectives lead them into political action from time to
time. In some cases, this may mean that a particular part of the
organisation has a special responsibility for political work. Consider the case of the Church of England. Its main purpose is that
of a religious organisation: to provide facilities, buildings and
clergy for worship and the administration of the sacrament in
accordance with its doctrinal beliefs, and to propagate its interpretation of the Christian gospel. However, it acts both as a sectional pressure group in relation to its own particular interests

and as a cause group on wider social issues. In relation to its own material and institutional interests:

> ministers and/or MPs may be lobbied in order to influence tax or other measures affecting the institution as employer or property owner: examples are continuing attempts to gain exemption from Value Added Tax on repairs to church fabric; efforts to get favourable treatment under the terms of the Land Bill . . . and, in 1987, efforts to recoup possible losses flowing from the proposed abolition of rates and their replacement by a community charge.
>
> (Medhurst and Moyser 1988, p. 313)

The Church also comments on broad social and political issues, although some politicians would prefer it to concentrate on redeeming the souls of its members rather than intervening in broader moral questions. Tensions with Mrs Thatcher's Government over a variety of issues ranging from urban regeneration to health service reforms 'partly reflect dismay, if not occasionally bewilderment, on the part of Conservative political leaders who have come to expect a generally supportive attitude from the established Church' (Medhurst 1991, p. 241).

Much of the Church's work with a political dimension is undertaken by specialist boards of the General Synod. The Board for Mission and Unity finds itself involved in issues relating to the Third World. The Board of Education has a more difficult task, as it is the link between the Church's network of schools and the Department of Education and Science. 'Whereas the Board may be perceived by the [Department of Education and Science] as a "peak association", able to negotiate authoritatively on behalf of Anglicans, those in Church House have in reality no real executive power vis-à-vis their constituents' (Medhurst and Moyser 1988, p. 329). The Board for Social Responsibility is perhaps the most politicised board, in part because 'its thinking on social policy is currently running counter to prevailing political orthodoxies' (p. 338). The prime purpose of the Church of England is, then, a religious one, but it has a secondary function as a pressure group seeking to influence public policy, albeit a rather special pressure group because of its status as an Established Church and the presence of bishops in the House of Lords.

Charities offer another interesting example. Their primary purpose is to collect funds in the pursuit of a defined charitable objective. They are unavoidably drawn into the political process because they are asked by government to offer advice on special policy areas such as the welfare of a particular category of disabled person; or because they act as agents for the dispensation of government funds (for example, Third World aid is increasingly dispensed through charities). Charity law prevents them from engaging in overtly political activity. They do, however, need to engage in such activity from time to time because, for example, changes in tax law can have a significant impact on their ability to raise and retain funds. Thus medical research charities have formed an Association of Medical Research Charities which is able to pursue public policy issues on behalf of its members. This is a clear example of a primary pressure group.

It is apparent from the discussion so far that there are many different types of pressure group. Writers on pressure groups have attempted to categorise the main characteristics of pressure groups through a variety of typologies. The next section presents an evaluation of the main alternative typologies.

Typologies of groups

A count of primary and secondary pressure groups in Britain which included locally based groups would almost certainly run into the tens of thousands (the Devlin Commission on industrial representation counted 1,800 business associations, which is only one of a number of categories). It is clearly not possible to study all these groups as individual organisations. Hence, a feature of the pressure-group literature over the last thirty years has been a variety of attempts to create typologies to classify groups, not only for descriptive purposes, but also in the hope that such typologies might lead to useful generalisations about their behaviour.

One of the most important distinctions has been that between sectional and cause groups. Sectional groups represent a section of the community. Their function is to look after the common interests of that section and their membership is normally restricted to that section. Cause groups 'represent some belief or principle . . . . They seek to act in the interests of that cause. Theoretically their membership is not restricted at all. Anyone can join and by doing so signify his acceptance of the belief or principle' (Stewart 1958,

p. 25). Sectional groups usually seek to organise as large a proportion of their eligible membership as possible. Their standing with government depends to a considerable extent on the validity of their claim to speak for a particular industry, group of employers or profession. Cause groups subdivide into those which seek a mass membership to take part in campaigning and those which seem content with a restricted membership, the implicit emphasis perhaps being on quality rather than quantity.

What useful generalisations does the sectional/cause distinction produce? First, it can be argued that the nature of the demands made by the two groups often tends to differ. Sectional groups are more likely to advance limited, specific goals which, as they are broadly coincident with the values of society as a whole, can be conceded without public controversy (see Jordan and Richardson 1987, p. 21). Sectional groups are often dealing with highly technical issues which do not interest the public at large, or which they would not understand. This does not mean that the resolution of the issue is unimportant to the members of the group concerned: it may have a considerable bearing on the profitability of an industry, or the future of a profession, but usually it will not become the subject of a wider public debate. 'On the contrary, a high-profile area such as nuclear policy or abortion or constitutional reform is unlikely to be resolved without wide participation and parliamentary legitimation' (p. 21).

It could be argued that sectional groups find it easier to recruit members because they appeal to a well-defined constituency with a particular interest at stake. (For a further discussion of this point in terms of Olsonian theory, see Chapter 2.) The research carried out by the Aberdeen group points to a high level of membership turnover among cause groups. Only 35 per cent of those who joined Friends of the Earth in 1991 rejoined in 1992, while Amnesty International lost 24.5 per cent of its existing membership, but still managed to increase overall membership by 16.5 per cent (Jordan, Maloney and McLaughlin, 1994b, p. 547). Even so, as Table 1.1 shows, the membership of environmental groups, especially the newer and more radical groups, has expanded rapidly over the last twenty-five years, a period when political party membership has been declining. Cause groups are thus not necessarily less well resourced than sectional groups, and even if they have less money, they have more enthusiastic activists willing to devote time and energy to the group's work.

Table 1.1   The growing membership of some leading environmental organisations (membership figures in thousands)

	1971		1992
Council for the Protection of Rural England	21		46
Friends of the Earth (England & Wales)	1		116
Greenpeace	30	(1981)	411
Ramblers' Association	22		94
Royal Society for the Protection of Birds	98		850
World Wide Fund for Nature	12		209

Source: Adapted from data in *Social Trends* 24 (1994) and reproduced with the permission of the Controller of Her Majesty's Stationery Office.

A classification of group strategies

The sectional/cause distinction is of some value as a first step in group classification. Dunleavy (1988) has developed an exogenous/endogenous distinction which, although similar in principle to the sectional/cause distinction, places greater emphasis on the development of group identities, i.e. subjective perceptions of interests shared with others. This distinction allows him to proceed to a richer and carefully specified set of implications about the decision to join a group, and group effectiveness, which will be returned to in later chapters.

However, there is also scope for a classification based on alternative group strategies, and on the receptivity of government to those strategies, which in turn has an impact on group effectiveness. One such classification is the insider group/outsider group division and its various subdivisions (Grant 1978). Insider groups are regarded as legitimate by government and are consulted on a regular basis. Outsider groups either do not wish to become enmeshed in a consultative relationship with officials, or are unable to gain recognition. Another way of looking at them is to see them as protest groups which have objectives that are outside the mainstream of political opinion. They then have to adopt campaigning methods designed to demonstrate that they have a solid basis of popular support, although some of the methods used by the more extreme groups may alienate potential supporters.

The insider/outsider distinction refers to a status that is achieved by the pursuit of a strategy. Strategy and status are very closely interlinked, so that pursuing an insider strategy is a precondition of winning insider status. This conflation of strategy and status has been criticised by Whiteley and Winyard (1987, p. 31) and more recently by the Aberdeen group. Jordan, Maloney and McLaughlin correctly argue (1992b, p. 17) that 'even if pursuing an insider strategy is a precondition to attaining the status, there can be cases where the strategy is not enough'. They suggest that 'the key variable is that of resources' which can cover 'knowledge, technical advice or expertise, membership compliance or consent, credibility, information, implementation guarantees' (p. 25). In their view:

> The logic of accommodation leads inevitably to certain behavioural norms. Grant's emphasis on the deliberate selection of behavioural norms then is an over-emphasis on the degree of choice.
> (Jordan, Maloney and McLaughlin, 1992b, p. 25)

While not denying the force of the logic of the bargaining process in a policy community, groups can make choices which can either improve an initially weak bargaining position or undermine an initially strong bargaining position. The National Federation of Retirement Pensions Associations (NFRPA), formerly the National Federation of Old Age Pensioners Associations (NFOPA), has seen its insider position deteriorate. From having an 'essential monopoly of organized pension reform advocacy in Britain' (Pratt 1993, p. 91) in the 1950s and 1960s when it met regularly with ministers, it has been outflanked by newer retirement organisations. The development of rival organisations reflected in part an assessment of the NFOPA's weaknesses. Age Concern decided to become more politically active after its then director had decided that NFOPA had 'failed to make a very significant impact on the national government' (Pratt 1993, p. 132).

The decline of the influence of the NFOPA in part reflected the diminished attraction of the social activities of its local branches as other leisure activities became available, often at discounted prices for older people. However, it also reflected choices made by the organisation. Because of the disruption caused by German bombing in the Second World War, the NFOPA moved its headquarters to Blackburn where one of its leaders lived, and they never moved back. In a centralised political system like that of Britain, effective insider groups need to be in, or close to, the metropolis:

the relative remoteness of its headquarters has not been without its cost in terms of NFRPA's political influence . . . the loss of . . . pre-eminence during the 1970s and 1980s was at least partially attributable to its physical remoteness from the center of British government.
(Pratt 1993, pp. 212–13)

Effective pressure-group activity increasingly depends on the ability to develop well-researched critiques of existing policy. As policy towards the elderly has become more complex, and developed new dimensions (such as those relating to nursing home care), the NFRPA 'has had difficulty adjusting given its lack of strong policy-analytic capability' (Pratt 1993, p. 136).

The Motor Cycle Action Group (MAG) provides an example of a group which has moved from outsider by necessity to potential insider status. At the end of the 1980s, the organisation faced serious difficulties. The newly elected chairman, Neil Liversidge, commented in his 1990 annual report that 'many people were writing MAG off as a shambles' (*Magnews*, August/September 1990, p. 6). This impression was confirmed by the public relations officer, who had been absent from the annual general meeting on a coast-to-coast ride in the United States, and also reported, 'I lost my home and my office facilities at the despatch company where I was employed which somewhat destabilised my power base to put it mildly' (*Magnews*, August/September 1990, p. 8). However, he also warned, 'Lobbying has to be organised along more disciplined lines with strict timetables that take account of political agendas.' (*Magnews*, August/September 1990, p. 8).

Improving the political standing of an organisation like MAG is not easy. As the Parliamentary Under-Secretary for Transport, Robert Key, who had accepted MAG's offer of 'a serious cross country bike ride', commented: 'they are great people . . . sometimes the image of motorcyclists is built up by the media, by films . . . as very macho, very aggressive and one of the things I like about MAG is that they perform a very useful function in the community' (*Magnews*, April/May 1994, p. 18). MAG has made a sustained effort in the 1990s to show 'that we are a serious pressure group that we really know what we're talking about' (*Magnews*, April/May 1994, p. 28).

This has been done in a way that has made effective use of limited financial resources. MAG still holds demonstrations in the form of mass bike rides, but it has placed an increasing emphasis on discussions with local MPs and the establishment of contacts with civil servants. Recognising the importance of the European dimension, it was involved in the establishment of a Federation of European Motorcyclists, with an office near Brussels staffed by a MAG member. In order to understand the operation of the EU, it sought free advice from political scientists, recommending a list of standard texts to its members. *Magnews* now contains references to, and discussions of, newly issued Commission documents. When it has held discussions with ministers, it has raised not only substantive issues, but also questions about how the consultation process is undertaken and who is included. Even if it still has to appeal to members with knowledge of French and German to help out with translation, it has shown considerable political sophistication in the way in which it has improved its bargaining position.

The value of the insider/outsider distinction is that it focuses attention on the choices that have to be made by groups and government, and on the exchange relationship that develops between them. The choices that have to be made by groups can be illustrated by the example of the animal protection movement, which exhibits a wide range of strategies. A very useful contribution to the pressure-group literature by Garner illustrates that the choice about what kind of strategy to follow is often rooted in fundamental moral choices. Garner draws a distinction (1993, p. 48) 'between those groups which emphasise animal rights and those groups which emphasise animal welfare'. Different moral orthodoxies produce 'the key division within the animal protection movement: between those who consider that animal interests should take a subordinate, albeit important, position and those who recognise a higher moral status for animals' (p. 49).

The animal protection movement exhibits every form of political action from the presentation to government of informed position papers to terrorist actions. The advocates of forms of direct action are not interested in bargaining with government, engaging in a dialogue with scientists, or influencing public opinion. They believe in acting directly to stop practices which they regard as morally reprehensible and because they see traditional pressure-group methods as having failed. They seek to damage directly 'the economic interests of those who use animals' (Garner 1993, p. 224). From their perspective 'insider status is not worth having given that the interests of humans, as producers and consumers, will always take precedence' (p. 209). Some radicals have, however, sought to work within the leading insider group, the RSPCA, to transform it from within. Although they had limited success, they did lead it to adopt a more active and controversial campaigning stance.

Groups have to make choices, but so do governments. Some kinds of demands and some forms of behaviour are simply unacceptable. Garner points out (1993, p. 208) that 'it is clear that the radical demands of the "rights" faction of the animal protection movement are not regarded as acceptable enough for government to consider granting it consultative status'. Christiansen and Dowding argue (1994, p. 16) that 'If it is government departments which decide which groups may receive insider status, then government is capable of allowing *only* those groups with which it sympathises institutional access to policy arenas.' It can be argued, however, that groups are able to use the media to influence public opinion to give particular issues a new priority on the political agenda. Governments have introduced environmental policies, however inadequate, in response to public concern and, once they have adopted such policies, they have to enter into relationships with groups who can provide information and expertise.

Groups enter into exchange relationships with government in which officials 'gain noticeable transaction benefits from what organized interests supply to policy-making' (Browne 1990, p. 500). As noted above, the NFOPA lost its insider status because it could no longer offer officials significant transaction benefits. The World Wide Fund for Nature is 'the classic example of an insider group which uses its conservation expertise as a means of gaining access to governments throughout the world' (Garner 1993, p. 203). If groups move towards more institutionalised and moderate stances, as has happened with Friends of the Earth and even to some extent with Greenpeace, they may be outflanked by new, more radical groups such as Earth First! whose members are prepared to take direct action such as sabotaging construction equipment used to build new roads.

A typology of insider and outsider groups

Jordan, Maloney and McLaughlin (1992b) suggest a new typology of insider and outsider groups which separates strategy and status.

This is suggested as a replacement for the original typology advanced by the author which divided insider groups and outsider groups as follows:

1. 'Prisoner' groups which find it particularly difficult to break away from government because of their dependence on government funding or because they are part of the public sector. McLeay suggests (1990, p. 628) that the police went through a process of politicisation which moved them from being a 'prisoner' group to a 'high-profile insider group' in a change of strategy reflecting 'increased demands placed upon them'.
2. 'Low-profile' insider groups working largely behind the scenes.
3. 'High-profile' insider groups who cultivate public opinion to reinforce their discussions with government.
4. Potential insider groups – outsider groups which seem to have the capacity to win insider status.
5. Outsider groups by necessity who lack the political sophistication to win insider status.
6. Ideological outsider groups who reject the existing political system because they do not think that meaningful change can be achieved through it.

Jordan, Maloney and McLaughlin suggest a threefold classification of strategies: insider, outsider and thresholder. This third category relies on May and Nugent's work which suggests that thresholders can be 'characterised by strategic ambiguity and oscillation between insider and outsider strategies' (May and Nugent 1982, p. 7), offering the trade unions as a principal example. A thresholder strategy can, however, be a high-risk strategy. The mixed strategy pursued by the unions helped Conservative governments to portray the unions as irresponsible bodies, and to diminish the status they had enjoyed as leading insiders.

In terms of status, Jordan, Maloney and McLaughlin divide insider groups into core insiders; niche insiders; and peripheral insiders. The distinction between core and niche insiders is essentially in terms of their range of concern, and the number of issues on which they are consulted. The Aberdeen group use the National Farmers' Union and the British Poultry Meat Federation as illustrations. Using American data, Browne suggests that 'the large number of interests in the agricultural domain give rise primarily to very narrow and intensely directed issues . . . . Policy interest is characterized by obsessive focus on a single facet of agriculture production and food delivery.' (Browne 1990, p. 489) In the United States, agricultural politics has been centred around particular commodities more than it has in Britain where there has been more aggregation of interests.

Quite how one might classify particular groups into the 'core' and 'niche' categories is not easy to decide. For example, McLeay's work on the police suggests that 'There is a simple and direct link between the Home Office and the police, mainly through regular meetings, joint working parties and consultations between ACPO [The Association of Chief Police Officers] and the Home Office.' (1990, pp. 626–7) Clearly ACPO are core insiders, but what of the Superintendents' Association: are they core or niche?

Any typology always poses assignment difficulties and the core/niche distinction introduced by the Aberdeen group is an interesting one. In any case, 'The real issue as we see it concerns the distinction between peripheral, and core and niche insiders.' (Jordan, Maloney and McLaughlin 1992b, p. 20) Peripheral groups are seen as marginal and relatively uninfluential participants in the policy-making process. 'Given the low threshold for entry into consultation lists we believe that most groups who wish insider status can, relatively easily, develop the necessary degree of political sophistication to attain peripheral insider status.' (p. 20) One can accept that getting on the consultation list is not difficult, but groups who want to be real insiders are unlikely to be satisfied with this kind of token access. According to the responsible minister, 200 groups are consulted on issues relating to motor cycles, and 5,000 on motoring issues, presumably meaning that they receive a circular letter from the department inviting replies (*Magnews*, April/May 1994, p. 17). The Motor Cycle Action Group would not have been satisfied with courier status: they wanted to keep their helmets off, and get upstairs to talk to the decision-makers, which is what they have done.

The Aberdeen typology is a helpful and intelligent modification of the original categorisation. Nevertheless, there is a value in maintaining a broad insider/outsider distinction, and it is important to be aware that transitional or marginal categories are just that. Groups have to decide whether they want to abide by the rules of the game and try and become insiders, or whether they want to remain outside the conventional political process. Although 'insider status, by itself, is not equivalent to influence' (Garner 1993, p. 193), most groups 'want to achieve access to government even if they will not admit as much' (p. 194).

The gains and costs of an insider strategy

Outsider groups as a category are by their nature more disparate than insider groups. The very fact of being an insider group imposes certain constraints and patterns of behaviour on a group. A group which does not abide by the rules may find itself excluded from the consultative process. Groups need to build a reputation of providing information that is accurate, well researched and not exaggerated, on which decision-makers can rely with confidence. This applies as much at the European Union level as in Britain. One study of Brussels lobbying found that a trade association which 'put forward incorrect arguments . . . were finally excluded from the consultation process; and an interviewee who categorically stated, "If I am fed false statistics, I close my door for five years."' (Burson-Marsteller 1991, p. 8)

The basic point about the insider/outsider distinction is that an interest group has to be able to deploy certain political skills before it can be accepted as an insider group. It has to show civil servants that it can, and is prepared to, talk their language; that it knows how to present a case, and how to bargain and accept the outcome of the bargaining process. The language of the British civil service is a language of veiled understatement and it is characteristic of politically unsophisticated outsider groups that their demands are often presented in strident and uncompromising terms.

In the longer run, most groups tend to veer towards an insider strategy because of the potential gains it offers. For example, Greenpeace has 'devoted more resources to research, to report-writing and to conventional lobbying techniques. These changes have in turn annoyed some of the direct action traditionalists, who fear loss of purity and effectiveness' (Edwards 1988, p. 18). Certainly, there are risks in exchanging independence for incorporation. Nettl argues that the 'British consensus' has the effect of emasculating pressure groups 'while preserving their outward shell of autonomy and independence' (Nettl 1965, p. 22). According to Elliott *et al.* (1982, p. 91), what used to be the National Federation of Self-Employed accepted incorporation as the price to be paid for durability. Even more established groups may feel that they have paid too high a price for access to government. Isaac-Henry (1984, p. 145) comments in relation to local-authority associations:

> Of course the associations must react to government initiatives, but they seem to be inexorably drawn into an all-embracing web of consultation which in essence makes them prisoners of the centre. There is a danger that when leading officials and members spend so much time with government officials and ministers they become servants of the centre, and their role is reduced to that of explaining government policy to member authorities.

Above all, an important point about the insider/outsider distinction is that it highlights the way in which the state sets the rules of the game for pressure group activity. Access and consultation flow from the adoption of a pattern of behaviour which is acceptable to government, particularly to civil servants. This creates incentives for groups to act in a particular way; pressure groups are thus tamed and domesticated with only the ideological rejectionists remaining outside the system.

Pressure groups and democracy

There is a fundamental link between the existence of pressure groups and the very survival of a system of democratic government. Freedom of association is a fundamental principle of democracy. Democracy permits the existence of groups, but it could also be argued that groups contribute to the quality of the decision-making process. Those that have axes to grind may have something to say that is relevant to the issue under consideration.

A system of representative democracy offers electors a relatively infrequent choice between alternative party programmes. Systems which permit referenda to be held on specific issues extend the range of choice, but one consequence is often that the protagonists spend large sums of money on advertising to influence the outcome, with an unfair advantage being given to the side with more money. Pressure groups permit citizens to express their views on complex issues which affect their lives. In most systems of voting, each vote (at least in principle) counts equally, but numerical democracy finds it difficult, without elaborate systems of weighting votes, to take account of the intensity of opinion on a particular issue. Democracy cannot be reduced simply to a head-counting exercise: it must also take account of the strength of feelings expressed, and of the quality of arguments advanced. Moreover, group membership and activity offers an additional mechanism for citizens to participate in 'the experience of ruling and being ruled' (Lively 1975, p. 117).

This rather benign view of pressure-group activity can be challenged in two ways. It can be argued that pressure-group activity simply reinforces existing patterns of political inequality in society. For example, consider the position of business in society. Business already has considerable influence over people's everyday lives because of the economic assets at its disposal, assets which allow it to make decisions about the location of plants, the range of products to be produced, the numbers and types of persons to be employed, etc. Business is able to reinforce this economic power through pressure-group activity, either at the level of the individual organisation, the firm, or through organisations representing particular industries or business as a whole.

Why is business allowed this dual advantage? At a fundamental level, it could be argued that it reflects a value choice by society, expressed through the outcome of elections, in favour of a capitalist, free-enterprise society. In that society, businesses are corporate citizens, paying taxes and being required to obey a wide variety of laws and regulations. It therefore does not seem unreasonable that business should be allowed an opportunity to express its views on public policies that affect it. On a practical level, it should be noted that there are two additional reasons why governments consult business interests. First, business can advise government on the practical consequences of a particular policy, thus helping government to avoid policies which are ineffective, or which have undesirable and unintended side-effects. Second, business is often called on to assist in the implementation of a particular policy, such as a training policy, making it desirable to maintain its goodwill.

Even so, it can be argued that pressure groups which represent organisations rather than individuals have certain advantages in terms of their ability to exert effective influence on public policy. An institution has interests that are independent of its particular members, and its leadership has greater latitude in making decisions about how those interests can best be served. 'Institutions have less need to justify their political efforts by reference to membership approval or demand' (Salisbury 1984, p. 68). The significance of groups organising institutions is apparent when one considers that Rhodes *et al.* (1981) identified twenty-two associations representing local authorities, ranging from the Association of County Councils to the Federation of British Cremation Authorities.

More generally, it is evident that groups which represent producers are usually more effectively organised than those which represent consumers. Contrast, for example, the organisation of business with the weakness of general consumer organisations; or the organisation of doctors with that of patients. This is not surprising when one considers that there is not really a consumer interest: rather, individual consumers have a wide range of interests flowing from their own particular needs and perspectives. For example, consider attitudes to public transport. Some consumers may prefer a market-oriented solution such as privatisation of British Rail, others may prefer an increase in subsidies to public transport. Among the latter group, a regular user of Network South-East or the London Underground is going to have rather different priorities from those of a person who wants the bus service to his or her village restored, or who uses a publicly run shipping service to the Outer Hebrides.

Such problems make consumers difficult to organise. Indeed, in some respects, this difference is a reflection of the extent to which groups are used to convey intensity of opinion. A farmer whose livelihood is threatened is likely to be more concerned about a new dairy regime than a consumer faced with paying an additional penny for a pint of milk.

One should not, however, dismiss too readily the concerns which have been expressed about the tendency for at least some pressure-group activity to reinforce existing concentrations of power. However, it is difficult to take a position on these issues without having some general theoretical perspective on the role of pressure groups in the policy-making process, and a number of alternative theories are set out in Chapter 2.

The other challenge that has been mounted to pressure groups questions their impact on the overall decision-making process in a society. In summary, it is argued by some liberal writers that the presence of what are referred to as 'vested interests' makes it difficult to bring about necessary changes in a society. By mounting an effective defence of the status quo, group activity leads to ossification in a society. At the opposite end of the spectrum are the prescriptive corporatists who argue that a close relationship between groups and government is not only the most effective way of governing a polity, but also one that contributes to social progress. These alternative perspectives will also be considered more fully in Chapter 2.

2

Pressure groups and the political system

This chapter reviews a number of alternative theoretical perspectives on the place of pressure groups in the political system. The focus is on theories which help us to understand the role of pressure groups in the democratic political process as a whole. Theories which consider, for example, the problems of recruiting or retaining group members, or the internal dynamics of interest groups, will be discussed only insofar as they are relevant to these broader issues.

One important point to bear in mind when reading about the various theories is the distinction between *analytical* and *normative* theories. There is, of course, a sense in which all theories are normative because the process of theory formation is not value free. Even so, a distinction can be maintained between those theories which set out to describe and explain a particular set of political phenomena, and those which seek to prescribe a preferred set of political arrangements: the distinction between 'is' and 'ought'.

One of the problems with pressure-group theory is that this distinction between analytical and normative theories has often not been maintained, or at least has become confused in the minds of those writing about the subject. Consider corporatist theory, which is discussed more fully later in the chapter. Many of the writers on corporatism are prescriptive corporatists, that is, they believe that neo-corporatist arrangements enhance the quality of decision-making in a democratic society, and that countries with such arrangements are, in general, better off than those without them. Other writers have been interested in corporatism simply as a means of trying to understand changes which took place in the relationship between the state and pressure groups in a number of western societies in the post-war period. They are not arguing that corporatist arrangements are particularly beneficial: simply that they have occurred, and need to be studied if we are to have a better understanding of the democratic process. However, the distinction between these two approaches often becomes blurred, so that analytical writers on the subject are often labelled corporatists along with the prescriptive corporatists.

Pluralism

Pluralism offers the most influential and resilient account of the role of pressure groups in a democratic society. In part, its resilience is due to its elasticity: pluralists hold a variety of positions, particularly on the role of the state in a democracy. Jordan complains, 'Since pluralism is so vague a set of ideas it is difficult to understand how opponents can have rejected it with such confidence.' (1990, p. 286) This vagueness does, however, undermine the theoretical claims of pluralism, even if it makes it easier to deflect criticisms from any quarter.

One of the key characteristics of pluralism is the emphasis placed on the role of pressure groups in society as a means of providing access to the political system, and as a counterweight to undue concentrations of power. Thus, 'The pluralist case . . . rests on the argument that the essential thing is competition and participation among organized *groups*, not among individuals' (Presthus 1964, p. 19).

Pluralist theory is often caricatured by its less-informed critics, and it must be emphasised:

> Despite the accusations of many critics, pluralists do not see all pressure groups as having equal access to the policy process . . . pluralists accept that relationships between interest groups and government agencies can become very exclusive . . . . Pluralists do not expect a free flow of groups and ideas into the policy arena, nor do they regard all groups as having equal access and power.
> (Smith 1990a, p. 303)

Pluralist theory combines within it a mixture of normative and analytical elements: pluralist theorists often seem to be simultaneously offering both an account of how society ought to be organised, and a working model of how society is actually organised. In this description, pluralism will be treated as an analytical theory, but it should be emphasised that it has considerable normative undertones.

Pluralists believe that power in society is fragmented and dispersed, a 'system of dispersed inequalities' (Jordan 1990, p. 288). In particular, they believe that power is non-cumulative in the sense that those who are powerful in one arena are not necessarily powerful in another. This idea of distinct issue areas has given rise to the neo-pluralist notion of policy communities, which is discussed more fully below. The dispersal of power is assisted by the presence of a large number of groups, and by the existence of a rough balancing equilibrium in the society which operates through the presence of countervailing groups, e.g. labour countervails capital. If a particular interest is neglected, then a 'potential' group will be mobilised to represent it (see Truman 1951). This theory does have some practical relevance: in research on the CBI, Marsh and I discovered that its members thought that a principal reason for its existence was the need to provide a counterweight to the Trades Union Congress, a consideration mentioned by almost every director we interviewed (Grant and Marsh 1977, p. 49). However, Smith (1993, p. 27) makes some telling criticisms of the notion of potential groups:

> It seems likely that potential groups are those that have great difficulty organising, such as consumers or the elderly, who do not meet collectively, lack resources, often have conflicting interests and lack economic power. However much their interests are threatened, they are unlikely to become actual groups. Indeed the concept of a potential group is questionable. How can a potential group exist when the concept group involves some form of collective identity? A group can only exist once it is formed.

It is important to bear in mind that 'The major literature on pressure groups is American. There is no major British contributor to theory' (Jordan and Richardson 1987, p. 53). (A subsequent exception is Dunleavy 1988, 1991.) One consequence of this is that pluralist theory often seems to reflect a more open, fragmented political system than applies in the case of Britain. In particular, government is often presented as highly fragmented. Such a picture has considerable validity in the USA with its autonomous executive agencies, but less so in Britain. However, the notion of policy communities has been developed largely by British theorists, and may offer a more accurate portrayal of the key features of the pressure-group system in Britain.

Pluralism: an assessment

Much of the pluralist case rests on the assumption that access to the political system is relatively easy, that forming a group which will be listened to is not particularly difficult. In 1965, Mancur Olson published a book called *The Logic of Collective Action* which cast doubt on some of the central assumptions made by pluralists in 'an apparently devastating critique' (Dunleavy 1988, p. 23). Olson argued that there was a logical flaw in the pluralists' treatment of economic interest groups. They assumed that individuals in a large group would make sacrifices to attain the political objectives of the group. Olson pointed out that the individual member of a large organisation was in a position where 'his own efforts will not have a noticeable effect on the situation of the organization, and he can enjoy any improvements brought about by others whether or not he has worked in support of his organization' (Olson 1965, p. 16). Olson argued that the relatively small groups, which he termed 'privileged' or 'intermediate' groups, would be much easier to organise:

> The small oligopolistic industry seeking a tariff or tax loophole will sometimes attain its objective even if the vast majority of the population loses as a result. The smaller groups – the privileged and intermediate groups – can often defeat the large groups – the latent groups – which are normally supposed to prevail in a democracy.
> (Olson 1965, pp. 127–8)

Olson explained the existence of large numbers of groups in terms of a by-product theory of pressure groups. Members did not join because of the collective goals the groups pursued, but because of the selective incentives (services, discounts, etc.) which were available only to members. Olson drew a picture of the pressure-group system in which the business community was by far the best-organised sector. It should be noted that Olson admitted that his theory did not apply to 'philanthropic' groups, where those organised were concerned about persons other than those in the group itself. It is in this area, of course, that there has been a considerable expansion of group activity since Olson wrote his book. As Jordan asks (1994, p. 17), 'Does Mancur Olson visit a bottle bank?' His answer is that, as visiting the bottle bank is not economically rational as it incurs costs without any return, 'Presumably Olson puts his in the bin.' (p. 22)

It would be no exaggeration to say that in the years after the publication of Olson's book, the study of pressure groups lived through 'the Olsonian years'. At the session on pressure groups at the Political Studies Association conference at Swansea in 1994 Olson's work provided much of the focus of the discussion, although six years earlier at the 1988 annual meeting of the American Political Science Association it had been observed that there was now a need in the study of pressure groups to move 'beyond Olson-type questions'.

In the decades since Olson's book was published, pressure groups have continued to multiply. This is, of course, what Truman argued in terms of a proliferation thesis. As processes of economic and social differentiation took place, more grounds for group emergence appeared (Jordan 1994, p. 3). Walker observes that 'the recent increase in the number of groups suggests that Truman has the data on his side', while admitting that 'An increase in the number of groups, by itself, would not disconfirm Olson's theory.' (1991, p. 75). How can this increase be explained in Olsonian terms? Dowding is sceptical of the by-product theory, arguing that 'selective incentives cannot be the primary incentive for members of an organization primarily devoted to lobbying' (Dowding 1994a, p. 542). This observation is supported by the survey work undertaken by the Aberdeen group. In the case of Friends of the Earth, '86.2% of existing members claimed that they would rejoin if direct member services were reduced, but only 31.5% would remain in membership if core campaigning was reduced' (Jordan 1994, p. 12).

In many cases, of course, the cost of joining a group is so small relative to an individual's income or a firm's turnover that the decision to join falls below the rationality threshold. Deciding whether to join could consume more resources in terms of opportunity cost than the actual cost of joining. There is, moreover, an important distinction between membership and participation. As Moe points out, 'An individual may, for instance, derive a sense of satisfaction from the very act of contributing, when he sees this as an act of support for goals in which he believes' (1980, p. 188). Participation involves much higher costs in terms of the time expended by an individual or an employee attending meetings in the firm's time, but it also brings greater benefits with it: the solidaristic benefits of participation, and privileged access to a shared exchange of information. The former is generally of greater importance in cause groups, the latter in sectional groups.

Work in the United States by the late Jack Walker suggests that the Olsonian dilemma may be resolved by groups locating sources of funding outside their organisation. Walker focuses in his work on the role of external patrons of political action such as the federal government, major institutions and, most significant in the case of American citizen groups, wealthy individuals who 'are still a crucial source of the venture capital needed by aspiring political entrepreneurs' (Walker 1991, p. 81). Walker himself poses the question of whether this is a distinctively American phenomenon, and uses French data to suggest that it is not. It would seem evident, however, that Britain has fewer independent foundations and wealthy individuals than the United States, but this does not mean that Walker's perspective is irrelevant. The Rowntree Trust did help Friends of the Earth by providing free office space in its early years, while Amnesty International benefited from a legacy (Jordan 1994, p. 16). The most striking example, however, is the Royal Society for the Prevention of Cruelty to Animals (RSPCA). Of a total income of £21.7 million in 1990, £17 million came from legacies and only £128,000 from subscriptions (Garner 1993, p. 46). Radical activists believe 'that the growing reliance on alternative means of income is a convenient means of preventing the influx of those who want to change the direction of the Society' (p. 45).

It could be claimed that Olson's theory should really only be applied to such economic interest groups as the organisations with which he was concerned in 1965 and in his subsequent work. Assuming that he is not coerced by Maryland state law to separate his refuse, the question of whether he visits the bottle bank then becomes irrelevant. If, however, his theory is restricted to economic groups, Olson is 'no longer the missile aimed at the heart of pluralism' (Jordan 1994, p. 25). Olson's work does, however, provide an explanation of the special advantages that business enjoys in press-ure politics. 'Where businesses do have to join together, the bene-fits of their actions are often enjoyed by a small number of firms and so the incentives to organise are high.' (Smith 1993, p. 27) There are, of course, other ways of arguing that business enjoys a special position of power (Lindblom 1977), but Olson provides a formal model which exerts a particular influence given the growing popularity of public choice approaches.

Offe and Wiesenthal (1985) have argued that there are 'two logics of collective action'. Labour is powerless unless it organises: organised action is only one of a number of alternatives open to employers. Labour has been able to organise, but when groups such as the unemployed, the homeless and those in prison attempt to organise, they face special difficulties. Outside patronage may be difficult to obtain (Walker 1991), but the individuals in these categories may consider that their needs will be misinterpreted by well-meaning professional outsiders who have not shared their particular experience. 'The flaw in the pluralist heaven is that the heavenly chorus sings with a strong upper-class accent' (Schatt-schneider 1960, p. 35).

Another set of problems arises from the absence of democracy within many pressure groups themselves. Either arrangements for democratic control are limited, or they tend to fall into disuse. Control of an organisation can pass into a self-perpetuating oligarchy. Activists tend to be those who have the time and money to devote to organisational work, so that doctors' organisations may have a disproportionate number of doctors with private prac-tices in leadership positions, whilst farmers' organisations may be led by the better-off arable farmers who can afford to be away from their farms. However, such leaderships must be careful not to move too far away from the opinions of their members, or they may lose large segments of the membership, as, for example, in the case of the separate organisation of a Welsh Farmers' Union.

A more fundamental criticism of pluralism is that there are two levels of power in society, and that pluralism really only tells us about the lower level. The upper level is that of the core assump-tions of society, such as private property, which largely go unques-tioned. These core assumptions set the terms of reference for conflicts and outcomes at the lower level where 'the picture will look something like the polygon of forces found by pluralist analysis' (Westergaard and Resler 1976, p. 248). It could be argued, however, that if the core assumptions of society are to be challenged, it should be done through the party system where electors can be offered a radical alternative to the status quo such as that offered by the Green Party. Within government itself, the battle for resources between different departments does, in some senses, resemble a competition between particular institutionalised interests (health, education, industry, agriculture, etc.).

Policy networks and policy communities

The notion of a policy community represents a useful adaptation of the pluralist notion of distinct issue areas to the particular circumstances of modern British government. As originally developed by Richardson and Jordan (1979) it argued that the policy-making map was made up of a series of distinct vertical compartments, generally organised around a government department and its client groups, and largely closed off to the general public:

> The term 'community' was chosen deliberately to reflect the intimate relationship between groups and departments, the development of common perceptions and the development of a common language for describing policy problems.
>
> (Richardson 1993, p. 93)

In its original form, the idea was parsimonious and thought-provoking. In subsequent work, it has been complicated and sometimes diluted. As Judge notes (1993, p. 121), 'As more researchers joined the empirical field, so adjectival proliferation came to characterise the discussion of the concept, so replicating the same process that had occurred in the previous decade over corporatism.'

The idea of policy networks and policy communities has almost become part of the orthodox conventional wisdom of contemporary political science. Political scientists working on a variety of policy arenas have felt obliged to produce a map of their policy community as a first step in their analysis. This was accompanied, however, by a great deal of rather fruitless argument about what was a policy network and what was a policy community, showing once again that political scientists with a definition are rather like a dog with an old bone: they will not let it go, even if every morsel of nutrition has been extracted from it. Dowding (1994b) criticised the whole approach as representative of an informal descriptive empiricism characteristic of British political science which failed to address deeper questions which could only be approached through a theory of power.

The resulting debate at the 1994 conference of the Political Studies Association was as vigorous as it was inconclusive. Perhaps the most interesting point to emerge was that political scientists have been generally reluctant to discuss the normative implications of empirical research into policy communities. The analysis here will confine itself to considering how the notion of policy networks and policy communities can assist the understanding of pressure groups in Britain. In other words, the policy community approach will be treated as, at best, a model which might help us to understand the policy process.

As far as terminology is concerned, the discussion here follows what has become the dominant Rhodes–Marsh line. Policy communities are seen as a subset of policy networks used as a generic term to refer to organisations connected to each other by resource dependencies. Different types of networks can be placed along a continuum in terms of their degree of integration:

> *Policy communities* are networks characterized by stability of relationships, continuity of a highly restricted membership, vertical interdependence based on shared service delivery responsibilities, and insulation both from other networks and, invariably, the general public (including Parliament) . . . . These policy communities are normally based on the major functional interests in and of government – for example, of education and fire.
>
> (Rhodes and Marsh 1992, p. 13)

The Aberdeen group provide a useful summary of the central assumptions of the policy community model which they enumerate as follows (Jordan, Maloney and McLaughlin, 1992c):

1. Complexity in policy-making so that 'policy emerges from a complicated interaction of parties, political groups, and bureaucrats' (p. 4).
2. Lack of state autonomy, given that the policy community idea is based on an exchange between bureaucrats and interests.

3. Segmentation so that 'policies are made in sectors effectively restricted to those with an interest' (p. 7).
4. Civil servants are key policy-makers and develop mutual support relationships with pressure groups.
5. Relations are based in mutual trust.
6. There is an exchange-based relationship between civil servants and groups which encourages consensus-seeking.
7. Order and routine decisions. 'Both sides' experience leads them to narrow their expectations to areas where accommodation is possible.' (p. 13)
8. 'Most of the content of policy community discussions tends to be minor for society as a whole – but vital to participants.' (p. 14)
9. Restricted consultation so that 'a policy community can be seen as a mechanism for the assimilation of "legitimate" competing values and the exclusion of those competing values deemed "illegitimate"' (p. 18).

The relevance of the idea of policy communities can be illustrated by reflecting for a moment on health and agricultural policy-making. The president of the National Farmers' Union (NFU) and the general secretary of the British Medical Association (BMA) are key actors in the agricultural and medical policy communities respectively. They will have intensive contacts with ministers and senior civil servants in the Ministry of Agriculture, Fisheries and Food on the one hand, and the Department of Health on the other. However, if the general secretary of the BMA attempted to intervene in the fixing of intervention prices for dairy products, s/he might be deemed to require help from professional colleagues practising psychiatric medicine. Even if s/he were trying to argue that high levels of butter consumption are bad for public health, this might be seen as making an unwarrantable intrusion into matters not of his/her concern. Equally, if the president of the NFU expressed an opinion on the working hours of junior doctors, some of his/her own members might suggest an early rest cure. Policy-making is highly compartmentalised and this tendency has been increasing with the growing intrusion of highly technical matters into the policy-making agenda, particularly stimulated by the expanding importance of the EU.

It must be emphasised that the notion of a community does not imply that there is an absence of conflict, any more than there would be complete and undisturbed harmony in a geographical community. In their classic study of the Whitehall village, Heclo and Wildavsky note (1974, p. xv) that 'Community refers to the personal relationships between major political and administrative actors – sometimes in conflict, often in agreement, but always in touch and operating within a shared framework.' It must also be emphasised that policy communities differ from one another in their characteristics. Cox, Lowe and Winter (1986, p. 16) characterise 'The policy community for rural conservation . . . as large, diverse and pluralistic; that for agriculture as small, tightly-knit and corporatist'.

As an analytical proposition, the idea of policy communities clearly provides a good fit with the available empirical evidence on how decisions are made in British government. The existence of such policy communities does, however, raise some worrying problems for normative democratic theory. It is clear that these policy communities have rather high entry barriers around them (although the entry barriers are probably higher in longer-established communities such as agriculture than in younger ones such as conservation). Policy communities can become rather exclusive networks made up of well-established insider groups. Richardson and Jordan comment (1979, p. 174): 'One cost involved in the increasingly close relationship between groups and government is that the policy process has if anything excluded the general public from any effective influence.' What emerges is rather like an élite cartel in which participants collude to preserve the existing parameters of the policy-making process. Not only is the range of participants limited, but there are good grounds for concern about the quality of the decision-making process. Stringer and Richardson (1982, p. 22) argue that 'The objective of the policy-making process within these communities is often not the solving of real problems, but the management of avoidance of conflict, the creation or maintenance of stable relationships, and the avoidance of abrupt policy changes.'

Corporatism: yesterday's theory?

One of the problems about the corporatist debate was that there was little agreement about what the term meant. In its most basic form – tripartism – corporatism can be taken to refer to bargaining between the state, organised employers and the trade unions about the conduct of economic policy. The employers and unions were supposed to secure the adherence of their members to the agreements arrived at, thus reducing enforcement problems for the state.

Corporatist theory was attacked from all directions: by pluralists, who resented this attempt to invade their intellectual territory; by neo-marxists who regarded it as an inadequate theory, because of its pluralist roots and its failure to develop a theory of the state; and by Conservative politicians who saw corporatism as one of the major sources of British economic decline, even though Britain had experimented only with very weak forms of corporatism.

These battles are less relevant in the 1990s. Britain did move towards a limited form of corporatism under Conservative and Labour governments from the early 1960s until the end of the 1970s. In part this was because of the centrality of incomes (and, to a lesser extent, prices) policies in government economic strategy, leading to an emphasis on the development of effective bargaining relationships with the trade unions and employers. It quickly became apparent, however, that the employers and the unions in Britain both had difficulty in delivering their side of the bargain, even if they really wanted to. For example, with regard to one of the major tripartite agencies operating in the labour market:

> In the course of its history, the Manpower Services Commission found it increasingly difficult to achieve a consensus that required the corporatist partners to deliver their memberships, for example, for trade unions to accept a reduction in youth wages and a radical restructuring of apprenticeships and for employers to accept greater financial responsibility for training and retraining their workforces.
> (Ainley and Vickerstaff 1994, p. 543)

Thatcherism and corporatism proved to be incompatible, and the remaining tripartite institutions such as the National Economic Development Council (NEDC) were gradually abandoned, although it was John Major who finally got rid of an already weakened NEDC. This move away from liberal corporatism was not just a British phenomenon as, throughout the world, globalisation made it increasingly difficult for governments to adhere to a full employment commitment 'which many have seen as the underpinning of corporatist exchanges between states, capital and labour'

(Ainley and Vickerstaff 1994, p. 543). Paradoxically, it is state corporatism which has enjoyed something of a revival in the former Soviet Union and some of the former Communist countries in Eastern Europe.

As someone who would have to reply in the affirmative to the question 'Are you now, or have you ever been, a corporatist?', at least in the analytical sense, can any defence of corporatist theories be mounted? Has 'the negotiated mixed economy legitimised by corporatist frameworks . . . been largely discredited'? (Ainley and Vickerstaff 1994, p. 543) If a Labour government was returned in 1996 or 1997, would there be a reversion to tripartite arrangements? Certainly, the unions would occupy a more central place in the policy-making process again. However, they have been weakened by the loss of members, which is the result not just of government policies but also of far-reaching changes in the structure of the labour market. The employers, for their part, still show serious deficiencies of organisation, and have increasingly relied on direct company representation. A Labour government might have a more tripartite style, but only the reintroduction of an incomes policy would allow corporatist theories to be dusted down and re-examined to see if their shortcomings could be remedied.

The liberal critique of pressure groups

The study of pressure groups in Britain was pioneered by two American political scientists, Samuel Beer (1956, 1965) and Harry Eckstein (1960). Their starting-point was the American pluralist perspective on pressure groups, but they also found in Britain an older corporatist tradition which reinforced the legitimacy of group activity. Their view, then, of the pressure-group system in Britain was essentially a benign one, although Beer took a more pessimistic view in a later (1982) work. Their view was echoed by a leading British writer on pressure groups of the period, Sammy Finer (1958), who concluded his book with a plea for 'Light, more light!' – that is, more information and openness about the operation of the pressure-group system.

This benign view happened to be reinforced by wider developments in political life. The year 1960 saw the so-called Brighton Revolution, named after a major conference on the economy held in the town by the then Federation of British Industries. This marked a shift towards a more interventionist approach to the management of the economy which went beyond the aggregate demand management of the 1950s. (For an excellent analysis of this shift, see Hall 1986, Chapter 4.) Held against the background of increasing concern about Britain's economic performance, the Brighton conference led to a new enthusiasm for a limited form of economic planning among business leaders. (An excellent short account of the Brighton Revolution and its consequences is to be found in Brittan 1964, pp. 238–45.)

The significance of what developed into a shift to incomes policies and industrial policies was that it necessarily involved government in a closer relationship with key producer groups. The role of incomes policy in encouraging a tripartite style of government–industry relations has already been mentioned earlier in the chapter. Sectoral industrial policies usually draw government closer to pressure groups because their success 'is dependent on how readily producer groups will agree to accept the inevitable dislocations associated with economic adjustment' (Atkinson and Coleman 1985, p. 27).

The 1970s saw the collapse of the post-war Keynesian consensus, and its eventual replacement by a new monetarist orthodoxy. The exact reasons for this collapse do not concern us here, nor does the timing of the collapse or the extent to which the 1974–9 Labour Government repudiated Keynesianism. (For a fuller account, see Grant 1993b.) The first oil shock of 1973, alongside serious industrial disputes in Britain, precipitated the crisis of Keynesianism, but it can be argued that these particular events simply revealed more fundamental flaws in Keynesian political economy. Against a background of considerable economic and political disruption, constituting the most serious crisis in Britain's post-war history, a new critique of pressure groups developed.

This background has been sketched in to suggest that the time was ripe for some new thinking about the durability and viability of the post-war political settlement in Britain, which had involved a new emphasis being given to the role of pressure groups, particularly trade unions, in the political process. Indeed, a general debate about British 'ungovernability' was sparked off, although this has not stood the test of time very well given that Mrs Thatcher has shown that the British state has considerable powers at its disposal if it is directed by someone with strong and clear political convictions.

The most important piece of writing to appear at the time on the subject of pressure groups was an article by Samuel Brittan (1975). Brittan argued that liberal representative democracy was threatened by the generation of excessive expectations, and the disruptive effects of the pursuit of group self-interest. Producer groups had not in the past made full use of their potential power, 'but have tended to make increasing use of it as time has passed'. Brittan was particularly concerned about the activities of trade unions, which differed from other organised groups in terms of their willingness to withdraw output from the market until paid more. The kinds of demand being made strained to breaking-point the sharing-out function of democratic society.

The power of trade unions has diminished significantly since the 1970s, but Samuel Brittan has provided through his later work a more general critique of the role of pressure groups in democracy from the perspective of an economic liberal. His arguments are a healthy corrective to a period when extensive pressure-group activity was seen as an inevitable part of a modern democracy. Although he occasionally does have some good things to say about pressure groups, his perspective is based on a wish to defend the values of freedom and an open society. Reviewing an influential critique of pressure-group activity which he wrote in the mid-1970s (Brittan 1975), Brittan reflected (1987a, pp. 197–8):

> My theme . . . became the incompatible claims of rival interest groups which increase in influence when government takes on overambitious economic functions. Interest groups do not merely reduce the national income when they become embedded in the political process. They embody rival claims which more than exhaust the national product and threaten the survival of liberal democracy itself.

Brittan argues (1987b, p. 79) that interest-group pressure constitutes one of a number of threats to individual freedom and popular government. Analysing the interest-group threat, he notes (p. 74) that 'The main theme of Hayek's latest work is that democracy has degenerated into an unprincipled auction to satisfy rival organised groups who can never in the long run be appeased because their demands are mutually incompatible.' Brittan's clear message (pp. 262–3) is that 'the entrenched position of industrial, economic and political interest groups will limit what can be achieved by any form of economic management, new or old'. Constitutional and political reform is necessary to reduce the role of interest groups and increase that of the individual citizen.

It might appear that, with Mrs Thatcher's declared opposition to 'vested' interests, and her distaste for any kind of corporatism, the power of interest groups was fundamentally diminished. Certainly, the TUC – and even to some extent the CBI – became infrequent visitors to Downing Street. The implementation of policy continued, however, to be negotiated with affected interests, while the changes in policy-making that were introduced were not necessarily lasting. Under John Major 'there was a return to the more traditionalist style of policy-making in Britain . . . civil servants remarked that they now felt more able to return to a previous form of intimate dialogue with groups, less fearful of a prime-ministerial dictat' (Richardson 1993, p. 98). Even when Mrs Thatcher was in office, Brittan considered that Mrs Thatcher's Government had done very little to reduce certain areas of middle-class privilege. He notes: 'Many interest group privileges, for instance for pension funds, mortgage holders or concessions to farmers, appear as tax reliefs' (Brittan 1989, p. 17). Even in the privatisation programme, Mrs Thatcher's governments were very willing to make concessions to the existing managements of nationalised industries.

Another important contribution to the liberal critique of interest groups has been made by Mancur Olson (1982). Indeed, Brittan notes that 'There was a natural link between my thesis on collective pressures on democracy and the Mancur Olson thesis that the longer a country has enjoyed stable democratic political institutions, the more time there will be for interest group coalitions to form, which undermine performance' (Brittan 1989, p. 198). Olson argues that stable societies with unchanged boundaries tend to accumulate more special-interest organisations over time. The general effect is to reduce efficiency and aggregate income, and limit a society's capacity to reallocate resources and adopt new technology in response to changing conditions. Olson admits that a broadly based, 'encompassing' organisation has an important incentive to take account of the consequences of its actions on the society as a whole. He points out, however, that many of the 'peak associations' (such as the CBI and TUC) studied by political scientists lack sufficient unity to produce coherent policy.

Britain has a particularly powerful network of special-interest organisations, a phenomenon which Olson links to the country's poor growth record. 'British society has acquired so many strong organizations and collusions that it suffers from an institutional sclerosis that slows its adaptation to changing circumstances and technologies' (Olson 1982, p. 78). He concludes that special interests are 'harmful to economic growth, full employment, coherent government, equal opportunity and social mobility' (p. 237). One possible remedy might be the repeal of 'all special-interest legislation or regulation and at the same time [the application of] rigorous anti-trust laws to every type of cartel or collusion that uses its power to obtain prices or wages above competitive levels' (p. 236).

Much of what we know about the history of pressure-group activity would seem to support Olson's argument. The number of pressure groups has increased over time, and the exit barriers preserving groups tend to be higher than the entry barriers in the way of new group formations. It would also seem to fit in with much of what we know of inter-war economic history, particularly when viewed from the perspective of the institutional school of economic historians (Elbaum and Lazonick 1986). This was an important period in Britain's economic development because a recognition of the problem of poor British economic performance was accompanied by only partially successful attempts to do anything about it. Lazonick's (1986) study of the cotton industry, for example, shows what can only be described as an appalling degree of institutional rigidity, with structures shaped by Victorian moulds.

Olson's analysis is thus of value in pointing to a problem of political adjustment in countries like Britain. Older industries were able to develop a dense network of institutional protections (a 'well-developed, closed policy community', to use one language of analysis) which enabled them to slow down the transfer of resources to newer industries through protectionist measures, government subsidies, etc.

Where his analysis is more open to question is in relation to the argument that Britain was particularly afflicted by such problems. Just as some analysts tend to exaggerate the extent to which German industry was devastated by the Second World War, so Olson tends to overstate the institutional 'clean break' that occurred in

Germany and Japan (see Olson 1982, p. 76). Lynn and McKeown (1988, p. 173) argue that Olson very much exaggerates the extent to which special-interest groups were abolished in Japan under the rule of the militarists during the war and under the Occupation after it. Similar continuities may be observed in Germany (Grant, Paterson and Whitston 1988). A broader, cross-national study also suggests considerable elements of continuity in countries disrupted during the war by defeat or occupation (Grant, Nekkers and van Waarden 1991). In the case of Germany, van Waarden notes (1991, p. 297) that 'the war did not really entail a break in the development of structures of interest intermediation'.

The liberal critique of pressure-group activity has obliged those of us who take a relatively benign view of organised interests to re-examine some of our fundamental assumptions. The liberal analysis has helped to revitalise the analysis of pressure groups insofar as it was becoming increasingly focused on relatively narrow questions such as the merits of different typologies of pressure groups. Even if one does not agree with their particular analysis, writers like Brittan and Olson have made an important contribution towards lifting the debate on to a higher plane. They have redirected our attention towards broader issues such as the relationship between pressure-group activity and basic societal goals like the preservation of freedom and economic success. As Brittan (1989, p. 198) notes:

> The dilemma is that many of the same groups – e.g. trade associations, unions, farmers, clubs or users' councils – which appear in political theory as beneficent intermediate associations between the citizen and the state, and the very cement of democracy, appear in political economy as threats to economic performance and stability.

The Tory defence of interest

The liberal critique of interest-group activity, imperfectly reflected in Thatcherite thinking and action, stands in strong contrast to the traditional Tory analysis of the role of interest organisations in society. This traditional Tory or moderate Conservative strand was once the dominant tendency in the Conservative Party, but was supplanted after 1979 by Thatcherite neo-liberalism. Under Mr Major, the Conservative Party in Parliament has become seriously factionalised, particularly on the question of Europe, and no one tendency seems to be dominant. Michael Heseltine, once seen as the standard-bearer of 'one-nation' conservatism, is perceived to have shifted more to the right.

Tories reject the atomistic individualism inherent in neo-liberalism, and see interests as necessary and desirable intermediaries between the individual and society as a whole. Whilst not accepting Mrs Thatcher's view that there is no such thing as society – that is, that society is a totally artificial construct – they would argue that the individual cannot experience society as a whole. Organisations which link the individual to a wider community are valuable both for engendering a corporate spirit and for the communal good that they achieve. Indeed, the traditional Tory view comes close to being a prescriptive corporatist one, with its emphasis on the role of interests in governance and proposals for an 'industrial Parliament'. (This is a recurrent Conservative theme: see Churchill 1930; Amery 1947; Gilmour 1983.)

The most articulate exponent of the Tory interpretation of interests in the 1970s and 1980s has been Lord Gilmour (formerly Sir Ian Gilmour). He argues that 'Tories were never enthusiasts for laissez-faire with its glorification of individual self-interest and its distrust of groups' (Gilmour 1983, p. 203). 'A Tory, then, rejects the simple idea that individuals are selfish and good and groups selfish and bad' (p. 204). That is not to say that Gilmour views all groups benignly. He was very critical of the British trade union movement, arguing for the need 'to make trade-union activity less self-destructive and to bring home to the average trade-unionist that union power is only legitimate within limits' (Gilmour 1978, p. 239). However, he has also been very critical of the CBI, which he portrays as weak, divided, lacking in political intelligence and sophistication, and subservient to the Conservative Party (Gilmour 1983, pp. 194–5, 207). More generally, Gilmour echoes earlier arguments about the role of interest groups by arguing that their activities should be made more visible, with greater democratic influence being exerted over them (p. 208).

Socialist views of pressure groups

There is not really a distinctive socialist view of pressure-group activity, although there is obviously a strong suspicion of business interests, particularly multinational big business. Centre-left post-war Labour governments in Britain, because of their wish to manage the economy, have tended to veer towards a weak form of prescriptive corporatism. This has been marked by intensive consultations with the unions and the employers, although all the major tripartite institutions were set up by Conservative governments. There have also been some half-hearted attempts by Labour governments to improve the position of underorganised interests, for example with the formation of the National Consumer Council.

In general, however, the impression that emerges from reading the many books by former Labour ministers is the extent to which they took an orthodox approach to pressure groups. That is to say, they viewed them as a legitimate part of the political system which had to be consulted, although this might often become a chore. They were certainly irritated by organisations which went outside the conventional channels and resorted to demonstrations. In general, however, they worked the system as they had inherited it, although developing it through closer partnership relationships with selected pressure groups.

A future Labour government might be expected to respond more favourably to various groups representing the 'dispossessed' in society: for example the homeless, those in poverty, those with disabilities, sexual minorities. Environmental groups might also get a more receptive hearing, particularly if the government was dependent on support from the Liberal Democrats. The imperatives of managing the economy would, however, necessarily draw a Labour government into a close relationship with economic interests, while efforts to improve the education and health services would lead to a dialogue with various professional producer groups. There would thus be continuity as well as change in relationships between the government and pressure groups.

3

How pressure groups influence Whitehall and the political agenda

Pressure groups do not have the power to make authoritative decisions themselves. They do not constitute governments, or control legislatures, or staff courts. Hence, their success in achieving their objectives depends on influencing political institutions to adopt the policies and measures they advocate. This may involve securing the attention of political influentials, which could entail using the media to win public sympathy for the case advocated. Even so, it must be stressed that the bulk of pressure-group activity is very undramatic and routine, and is invisible to the public eye. It involves a series of detailed discussions with civil servants, MPs or peers about the content and implementation of legislation.

It should also be remembered that pressure groups spend a lot of time talking to other pressure groups. Sometimes this may be to try and build a coalition on a particular issue and thus strengthen a particular case being put to government. Alternatively, producer pressure groups engage in discussions with other groups with whom they are potentially in conflict. A trade association will usually have more or less formal arrangements for maintaining contacts with its suppliers and its customers. For example, food industry associations talk to retail associations about questions ranging from discounting to the conflict between 'own-label' and manufacturers' brands.

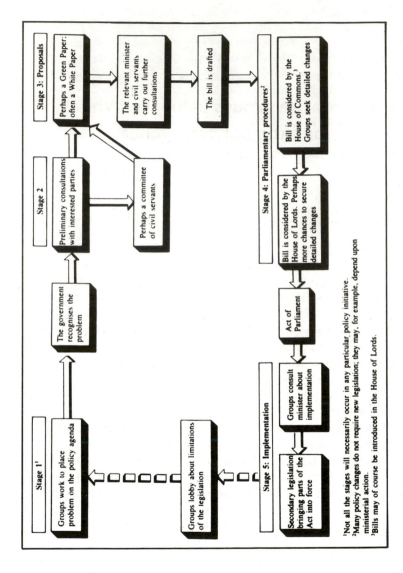

Figure 3.1 A simplified outline of group involvement in the policy process

[1] Not all the stages will necessarily occur in any particular, policy initiative.
[2] Many policy changes do not require new legislation; they may, for example, depend upon ministerial action.
[3] Bills may of course be introduced in the House of Lords.

There is no one route by which pressure groups exert influence. The general features of the process can, however, be presented in the form of a simplified flow diagram (see Figure 3.1). Not all the stages presented in the diagram will be relevant to every instance of a pressure group exerting influence. For example, some cause groups have been able to achieve their objectives through the passage of a private member's bill, as happened with abortion law reform and the abolition of capital punishment. There will be further consideration of the role of legislation in Chapter 4. However, many cause groups are more concerned to influence government rather than Parliament, for all insider groups issues will usually be pursued first through discussions with ministers and civil servants.

Getting issues on the political agenda

The political agenda is crowded, and there are limits to the number of issues which can be processed at any one time. This is reflected in the pressures on parliamentary time. Even under the Thatcher Government, which was supposedly committed to rolling back the influence of the state, each Queen's Speech contained a substantial amount of new legislation. The Cabinet and its Legislative Committee have to discuss which possible measures are to have priority in a particular session. During the year, there will have to be discussions about whether to offer minor concessions to speed up the passage of a particular piece of legislation, and when and where the guillotine should be applied.

However, important though the legislative agenda is, the political agenda is a somewhat broader concept. It refers to those issues which arouse public concern at a particular period of time. There may be short-run variations in response to particular events, but there may also be longer-term shifts in public opinion. For example, security of employment was a greater concern for the electorate in the early to mid-1990s than in the late 1980s. The media undoubtedly play an important role, if not in creating public opinion then at least in reinforcing it. The rise in the importance of the environment as a political issue undoubtedly owed something to increased media attention. In part, this reflected the growth of television as a communications medium, particularly the introduction of colour television. Pollution disasters offer powerful visual images: a spreading oil slick; stunted trees; dying seals.

Some groups, particularly cause groups, may be seeking to establish 'their' issue on the political agenda or to give it a higher priority as a prelude to obtaining effective political action. Indeed, the emergence of a new issue may often involve the formation of new cause groups or coalitions of such groups (see the case study of food additives below). Some sectional groups may also wish to obtain public attention for their problems, for example teachers' organisations may wish to draw attention to problems of violence against teachers, or of increasing stress levels being experienced by school heads. Very often, however, sectional groups will want to keep issues away from public attention as much as possible, so that they can be processed through familiar consultative channels. Once an issue has been placed on the political agenda it 'passes into the relatively closed world of the executive departments of state and, to a lesser extent, interdepartmental and cabinet committees, where the consideration given to issues and possible responses by politicians and officials is still largely shielded from public gaze' (Solesbury 1976, p. 392). Media attention may soon switch elsewhere and, as Solesbury points out, there is a variety of 'partial responses' open to government which may reassure the public without eradicating the original problem (p. 394).

Interest groups can use the media to move an item up the political agenda. In general, however:

> The combination of national mood and election is a more potent agenda setter than organized interests . . . . [Interest groups] less often initiate considerations or set agendas of their own. And when organized interests come into conflict with the combination of national mood and elected politicians, the latter combination is likely to prevail, at least as far as setting the agenda is concerned.
>
> (Kingdon 1984, p.208)

A decreased ability to influence the content of the political agenda may reveal a weakening of a group's position. Smith notes that 'The farmers failed to keep the *salmonella* in eggs issue off the agenda' and sees this as 'indicative of a general weakening of the position of farmers' (1991, p. 244).

Even when a pressure group has the national mood on its side, it will find it difficult to overcome government resistance. The

RSPCA had widespread popular and legislative support, as well as the backing of other key groups such as the Police Federation, for its dog registration scheme. The Conservative Government defined the problem in terms of a scheme for a restricted range of dangerous breeds, being motivated not by animal welfare considerations, as the RSPCA was, 'but by a concern for human victims of the attacks' (Garner 1993, p. 82). Even though the Government's majority was reduced to three on a three-line whip, the RSPCA still lost (p. 194).

Food additives: a case study of issue emergence

This case study explores through an examination of food additives the way in which new issues emerge on the political agenda. It is not concerned with the issue of food additives as such, but with the process of issue formation. As background it is, however, necessary to mention briefly the main uses of additives in food manufacturing:

1. Preservatives help food to keep longer. Without them, wastage rates would be higher, and the range of goods that could be stocked would be more limited.
2. Emulsifiers are used to mix together ingredients which would normally separate, for example mayonnaise and salad cream could not be made without an emulsifier. Stabilisers prevent ingredients from separating again.
3. Flavourings are by far the largest category of additives, but they are used in tiny quantities and are rarely entirely artificial. More controversial are flavour enhancers which make existing flavours in the food seem stronger. Monosodium glutamate, which has been widely used, stimulates the taste buds.
4. Artificial colours are another controversial set of additives, particularly tartrazine E102 which was one of the commonest and was linked with some adverse reactions.

Everything we know about the environmental and consumer movement suggests that it draws its strongest support from middle- and upper-class groups, and this general conclusion is supported in the particular case of food additives by a study carried out by MAFF. Respondents in the AB and C1 social classes were more likely to name food additives as damaging to health than those in the C2 and DE groupings, although it should be noted that age differences were an even stronger differentiator on this question, with the 55+ age group taking a more benign view of food additives than those aged between 25 and 34 (MAFF 1987).

The MAFF study underlines the importance of media publicity in relation to issue emergence. Fifty-nine of the women interviewed were aware of recent publicity on the subject, 65 per cent remembering it as part of a television programme (p. 24). A series of structured discussions with six groups of different social compositions showed that 'Most knowledge was media led and so was highly dependent on issues which happened to be taken up, perhaps solely for their news value' (p. 24). Respondents could recall a number of items from television programmes such as *The Food Programme*, but 'Women's magazines and newspapers were also influential via their regular coverage of nutrition, diet and additives' (p. 45). This media interest in the subject had, however, been fostered by a number of books such as Erik Millstone's *Food Additives* and Cannon's *The Politics of Food*. Some respondents in the MAFF study had read *E for Additives*, written by Maurice Hansen, a leader of both British and European associations for health food manufacturers.

The emergence of new campaigning organisations

The 1980s saw the formation of a new range of groups concerned with food issues who initially came together in the Food Additives Campaign Team (FACT) in 1985. In an introductory statement issued in June 1986, this body claimed that 'the widespread use of additives is now a menace to public health'. One of the earliest groups working in the area – although it has now largely disappeared from view – was the London Food Commission (LFC), a British example of Walker's patronage theory. This body was originally established under the auspices of the Greater London Council (GLC). After the GLC was abolished, it received funding from a trust which outlived the council's demise. The LFC operated with a small staff, contracting researchers to prepare reports. These were often well prepared, if written from a particular perspective, and attracted considerable media attention, with newspapers often referring to the 'independent' LFC.

This is an area in which groups have proliferated, and a new coalition, the National Food Alliance (NFA), was formed in 1985 under the auspices of the National Council for Voluntary Organisations and re-organised in 1990. Thirty-six diverse groups are brought together in this umbrella group. Parents for Safe Food, formed in 1989, is one of the more radical groups. Its director came from the LFC, and one of its first actions was a high-profile march on Downing Street. Organisations concerned with medical conditions, or backed by particular sections of the medical profession, represent a significant grouping within the NFA. One example is the Coronary Prevention Group which seeks to cut coronary heart disease by bringing about changes in people's eating habits. It attempts to appeal to the enlightened self-interest of food firms and retailers. Action and Information on Sugars, set up in 1990 to alert consumers to the health risks associated with excessive sugar consumption, draws some of its support from the dental profession. Other organisations encompassed in the NFA include the Vegetarian Society, women's organisations such as the National Federation of Women's Institutes, and the principal trade union in the food sector, the GMB (formerly known as General, Municipal and Boilermakers). The breadth of the membership is illustrated by the presence of the Campaign for Real Ale and the National Federation of City Farms.

The Public Health Alliance (PHA), set up in 1987, has a broader agenda than food, but has worked with the NFA in a campaign to control food advertising targeted at children. The principal constituency of the PHA is to be found in local authorities, especially their health promotion units, but it also has amongst its membership trade unions and campaigning organisations such as Alcohol Concern and ASH. It provides a good example of Walker's patronage theory, with an initial administrative post being supported by Birmingham City Council and subsequently by South Birmingham Health Authority, with project funding being secured from charitable trusts.

One of the most interesting organisations in the NFA in terms of agenda-setting is the Guild of Food Writers. This body was formed in 1984 and sees itself as having a campaigning agenda. The way in which the media have handled food issues has changed in a way that is likely to alter perceptions of these issues, at least among readers of broadsheet newspapers:

> In the 1970s food writing was apparently confined in the broad-sheets to what has been called the 'ghetto' of women's pages . . . . From being a domestic topic appearing weekly on the women's page food and drink writing now has its own two or three page spread in the style and leisure parts of the weekend paper . . . . One conse-quence of this process has been the opening up of space in food pages for critical and political views on food as opposed to recipes and gourmet writing.
>
> (Miller and Reilly 1994, pp. 31–2)

The campaigning organisations did not have it all their own way, however. They were attacked by the then Agriculture Minister, John Gummer, in 1990 and at various times were labelled in the press as 'fascists', 'terrorists' and 'Leninists' (Miller and Reilly 1994, p. 27).

All this media attention had its effect, reinforced by a number of 'food scares'. The former permanent secretary of MAFF, Sir Mich-ael Franklin, recalled that until the late 1980s, as far as food safety issues were concerned, 'this aspect of the Ministry's work trundled along without too much publicity' (Franklin 1994, p. 5). Substan-tive and procedural changes followed:

> The media and sensation-seeking experts had a field day. Govern-ments had to react. A consolidating bill which had been slowly and quietly creeping its way up the legislative queue suddenly blossomed as the all-singing, all-dancing Food Safety Act of 1990.
>
> (Franklin 1994, p. 6)

Franklin recalls that MAFF was able to resist pressure to set up a separate Food Safety Agency, but there was an internal reorgan-isation of MAFF to establish a Food Safety Directorate. Not only did new regulations and codes of practice have to be written, but MAFF was forced in the direction of greater openness and a more broadly drawn policy-making community:

> The government has even been forced to relinquish its traditional preference for operating in secrecy and to be much more open with the scientific data on which recommendations (e.g. for pesticide use) are based and in consulting all the consumer and other interests about its proposals before they become law.
>
> (Franklin 1994, p. 6)

Not all the campaigning groups are content to accept insider status. Work by the Aberdeen group suggests that Parents for Safe Food are consulted by MAFF, but rarely respond to the consultation invitations because they prefer public campaigning. The director of the Coronary Prevention Group is quoted as saying, 'If you're a pressure group there's nothing as frightening as when people start agreeing with you' (*Marketing*, 5 September 1991, p. 14).

The campaigning groups, operating through the media, have changed the politics of food from a technical subject dealt with in a closed policy community into a politicised arena operating in a more open policy setting:

> It is clear that with the politicization of food and new entrants into the policy network, food policy-making is not what it was. The *salmonella* affair reveals the extent to which food has become a key political issue and how the once consensual food policy community has been more divided and more conflictual and much more open to new interests.
>
> (Smith 1991, p. 253)

The food manufacturers have not necessarily lost out commercially from this development. Products can be advertised as 'additive free' or made appealing in other ways to an increasingly diet- and health-conscious population. The growth of vegetarianism creates a new market niche for products for which it is possible to charge a premium price.

Moreover, changing the agenda is one thing; bringing about a change in outcomes is another. It is as well to remember that a significant minority of the population in Britain subsists on a less than adequate diet, usually because of poverty (Stitt and Grant 1994). Families living below the poverty line do not have the information, choices and campaigning influence available to middle-class consumers. Is enough attention paid to those whose health suffers because of a poor diet resulting from inadequate levels of income, compared to the alleged effects of food additives on, for example, hyperactive children? (The MAFF study shows that much folklore was circulating among parents on this question.) Groups concerned with food issues would say that they are worried about the particularly unhealthy diets of the least well off, but their problems require solutions in other policy areas such as higher state pensions and family benefits, rather than more food safety legislation.

One of the most recent general interpretations of the politics of food is offered by Mills (1992). To summarise his argument, his analysis shows that government's role in relation to food products has been essentially reactive in that it has relied on controlling cases where products became dangerous for one reason or another. Although diet-related issues were placed on the political agenda in the 1980s, there were many constraints on state action. Mills sees manufactured food being 'reformed gradually by MAFF but in ways that can be easily absorbed by industry' (p. 189). The methods of decision-making will remain largely the same so that 'the policy communities and networks will continue to make policy largely as before' (p. 191). This scenario could be substantially altered by only two factors: the partial greening of British politics (an emphasis on 'partial' which is surely correct) and the increasing integration of the European Union.

Lessons from the case study

A number of general lessons can be drawn from this case study:

1. In order for an issue to gain higher prominence, there has to be some underlying public concern or interest in the first place.
2. This public concern can be focused and intensified by the media, with specialist correspondents playing an important role.
3. The emergence of an issue is often associated with the formation of new cause groups, or of alliances of existing groups which may be both cause and sectional.
4. Issue emergence should not be confused with the achievement of a shift in policy, although getting the issue on the policy agenda is the first step towards that goal.
5. Campaigning groups can have the effect of increasing biases in the political system which focus on issues concerning highly educated and better-off sections of the population, rather than those on low incomes, although the two are not necessarily mutually exclusive.

Influencing the executive branch of government

The Devlin Commission on Industrial Representation argued that 'All executive policy and most legislation is conceived, framed, drafted and all but enacted in Whitehall' (Devlin Commission 1972, p. 5). This statement was an exaggeration when it was made; moreover, Parliament has almost certainly acquired greater influence since it was made. Even so, it contains a substantial element of truth. As a senior official of the National Farmers' Union has commented:

> Getting in early is a very important golden rule. We have a sort of intelligence role on behalf of the farmers to keep our ears to the ground to find out what new initiatives are being proposed and what legislation may be coming on with the object of influencing it from the outset . . . . Whatever it is we shall be wanting to take an interest from the earliest stage. There is no question that once a piece of legislation reaches Parliament you may be able to tinker around the edges, but the prospect of getting any significant changes at that stage are very remote indeed . . . . Therefore it makes it much more important to try to get it right before it ever enters Parliament.
>
> (Holbeche 1986, p. 46)

Insider groups will try to influence policy when it is at the formative stage by talking informally to civil servants and ministers. In this respect, membership of some of the large number of advisory committees maintained by government may be important. As Jordan and Richardson observe (1987, p. 185), 'Through regularized participation in these structures, groups are able to shape the definition and perception of problems, influence the political agenda in those policy areas of direct concern to them, and influence the perception and emergence of "practicable" solutions.' The more solidified the proposal becomes, the more difficult it is to change. Even once a consultative Green Paper has been published, there are limits to the extent to which government will be prepared to modify its policies; this is even more true in the case of a White Paper, which can be seen as a statement of the government's intentions. Of course, consultations will go on in between the publication of the White Paper and the presentation of a bill to Parliament. However, by this stage they will be increasingly formal and even ritualistic, and the government's room for manoeuvre without losing face will be seriously limited. As Bruce-Gardyne (1986, p. 152) explains in the light of his experience as a minister:

the safest solution for the corporate lobbyist is to fix his trade association, and then to watch his trade association fix the civil service.
For once the deal is done, the honour of the civil service is engaged.
If it then fails to deliver its Ministers bound hand and foot, it hangs
its head in shame. Whereas the lobby which converts the politicians
is inevitably confronted by the resistance of the civil service.

The structure of government

In understanding how insider groups influence policy at the formative stage, it is really necessary to start with the structure of
government itself. Policy communities tend to form around government departments, and pressure groups are often concerned
when departments are reorganised. For example, the roads lobby
was unhappy when the Ministry of Transport was incorporated
into the Department of the Environment in 1970. In 1976 a new
Department of Transport was created. 'The experience of the DoE
suggested that the transport community was not happy to form
part of an integrated land-use planning department, and possessed
the political power to withstand this assault from those campaigning for greater integration' (Dudley 1983, p. 113). Similarly, reports that MAFF might be merged into the Department of the
Environment or recast as a Department of Rural Affairs have
concerned the NFU, leading to denials of any such intention by
both Mrs Thatcher and Mr Major.

   Although most insider pressure groups will have contacts with a
range of departments, they tend to have particularly close contacts
with one department. Indeed, they may encounter difficulties in
establishing relations with departments with which they are not familiar. This is partly because each department is anxious to defend
its clients. For example, the Energy Department, before it was absorbed by the Department of Trade and Industry, tended to defend
interests of energy-producing industries against energy users. It is
also a reflection of the importance of departmentalism within the
culture of the British civil service. 'The distinctive culture of the
department is at least as important as the culture of Whitehall as a
whole' (Plowden 1985, p. 26). Whiteley and Winyard (1987, p. 94)
noted the existence of different 'house-styles' and bureaucratic cul-
tures from department to department, while a study of the chemical
industry found considerable differences in departmental attitudes
towards the industry (Grant, Paterson and Whitston 1988).

It is also important to take account of the relative importance attached to different functions within a department. Discussing the organisation of the Ministry of Agriculture, Fisheries and Food in the immediate post-war period, when there was a distinct Ministry of Food, a then senior official of a food-processing industry association has commented:

> All Ministers at Whitehall Place do from time to time assure the food industry of their awareness that they are Ministers of Food *too* but in recent times they have in reality been, according to party, an extension of Ministers of Consumer Affairs or simply Ministers of Agriculture and, perhaps, Fisheries. Their policies have, it is true, sometimes been of benefit to this or that part of the food industry but that has been almost entirely coincidental.
>
> (Stocker 1983, pp. 250–1)

This version of events received confirmation from the former permanent secretary at MAFF, arguing the general thesis that from the merger of the two departments in 1955 to the late 1980s

> food policy, if it existed at all, was very much the junior partner in the MAFF. This was so from the outset. Much as we pretended to our colleagues that it was a true merger of the Ministries of Food and Agriculture, in fact it was a takeover. For the rest of my official career (and I retired in 1987), agricultural policy was in the driving seat.
>
> (Franklin 1994, p.4)

Some interest groups may have a close relationship with a particular junior minister who is perceived as an advocate for their particular needs; indeed, they may have lobbied for the particular post to be established. Examples include the creation of a post of Minister for the Arts in 1964 – probably most successful as a means of promoting the arts under its first incumbent, Jenny Lee – and a Minister for the Disabled in 1974. This latter post was less successful under the Conservatives, with the minister in 1994, Nicholas Scott, being criticised by his own daughter (a campaigner for the disabled) for his role in killing off a private member's bill on the rights of those with disabilities. Part of his defence was that the supporters of the bill had failed to consult adequately with business groups about the cost of its implementation. Although the effectiveness of such ministers has thus been questioned, Theakston (1987, p. 161) points to the increased expenditure secured through their championing of their clients; their liaison work with organizations at arm's length from Whitehall, local authorities and interest groups, helping keep the government in touch with problems and views outside; and the consolidation of responsibilities within Whitehall achieved under them.

The dullness of lobbying

A few years ago the author was sitting in the reception area of a trade association. Two other people were there, and one, clearly unfamiliar with trade associations, asked the other, 'What do they do here?' The reply was, 'It's very dull really, collecting statistics, and talking to civil servants.' It has to be emphasised that most lobbying is a rather dull business carried on between two sets of bureaucrats. Pressure groups employ professional staff, usually structured on relatively hierarchical lines. They then go and engage in detailed discussions with other bureaucrats working for the civil service about the details of, for example, a statutory instrument implementing an EC directive. A lot of the negotiation takes place with relatively junior or middle-ranking officials. Miller notes (1990, p. 94) that 'the great proportion of administrative judgements made and communicated to the public are by officials who have been well trained in the largely fictional convention of Ministerial Responsibility'.

Most representations should thus be directed at a relatively low level of the administrative hierarchy. As one under-secretary is reported as commenting, 'Action is taken at the lowest level in the Civil Service at which it can be competently handled' (Public Policy Consultants 1987, p. 16). Busy permanent or deputy secretaries are not usually going to contradict the advice given to them by junior officials who know much more about the issue under consideration. A booklet on working with Whitehall prepared for the CBI notes: 'it is the senior executive officer or higher executive officer in charge of a section of a policy division whose work is most likely to be relevant to the businessman' (Coffin 1987, p. 32). Whether such advice is taken is another matter: Public Policy Consultants (1987, p. 15) found that 77 per cent of the ministers and officials in their sample thought that pressure groups suffered from a mistaken desire to take things to the top.

The frequency of contact will vary from one group to another. Whiteley and Winyard (1987, pp. 92-3) make a distinction between regular, periodical and infrequent contacts, ranging from day-to-day relations to a major meeting once a year. Similar distinctions would apply to sectional groups. However, it should be noted that a particular issue may lead to more intensive contacts than usual. For example, the Ice Cream Federation had more than its usual level of contact with MAFF while an EC directive on ice-cream was under consideration.

The process of consultation usually starts with the department sending out a proposal for comment to a range of groups. Lists are maintained for the purposes of circulating such documents; they are usually rather long:

> Consultation processes related to food labelling issues (according to the relevant civil servant) involve approximately 500 groups within which some 20 to 30 organisations are seen as particularly influential. But it would not be unusual for them to receive somewhere between 30 and 60 responses to a particular aspect.
>
> (Jordan, Maloney and McLaughlin 1992d, p. 19)

The civil service considers that it is better to over-consult than to under-consult. As one senior civil servant has commented:

> We consult on any proposal those organisations which seem to be representative of the subject or interests under discussion. It is a subjective judgement on every occasion but we work on the basis that we would sooner over-consult rather than under-consult because you cannot from our position judge the importance on occasions of a particular proposal to a particular group of people.
>
> (Quoted in Coates 1984, pp. 146–7)

The initial consultation process could be viewed as a trawling exercise in which not everything that is obtained will be of value. A further process of sifting and grading has to follow. Most of the meetings that take place will be between pressure-group representatives and civil servants, although occasionally ministers will become directly involved. When that happens the meeting will often be a rather formal, set-piece affair in which both sides state their positions. Indeed, one of the chores given to junior ministers is to 'receive a large number of deputations and delegations to save them going to the top minister' (Theakston 1987, p. 139). Sometimes such meetings seem to be held for the benefit of the vanity of the pressure group's members. One experienced director of a regionally based association told me after his retirement that his

members were great believers in delegations to London. He recalled, 'They would put their case bluntly to the minister – with
little effect – and the man from the *Yorkshire Post* would be waiting outside the building and they would say, "We told him!"'

The annual 'Budget representations', made by a variety of associations to the Chancellor, often seem to have a rather ritualistic
character, amusingly recalled by Bruce-Gardyne (1986, pp. 157–9).
He suspects that often the whole exercise is for the benefit of the
trade press photographer waiting on the Treasury doorstep. The
delegation is duly displayed 'to advantage over a story reporting
that they have "made the strongest representations" and "received a sympathetic hearing"' (p. 159). Nevertheless, lobbying
the Chancellor does sometimes lead to a favourable outcome,
from the point of view of the pressure group, in the Budget.

Even so, there are times when it is useful to involve the minister; often it may be more appropriate to approach a junior minister who is handling a particular area of policy. For all the
constraints and limitations that they face, 'It is indisputable that
in the 1970s and 1980s junior ministers in general have played
more significant roles and carried more weight in Westminster
and Whitehall than in the 1940s, 1950s and early 1960s'
(Theakston 1987, p. 79). More generally, as Whiteley and
Winyard note (1987, p. 93), 'the view that civil servants run things
and that the minister has to go along with this is an over-
simplification. Individual ministers were perceived to make a real
difference to outcomes.' Some key decisions, such as whether to
refer a proposed take-over bid to the Monopolies and Mergers
Commission, ultimately have to be made by the minister person-
ally, albeit on the basis of advice offered by his civil servants.
Such decisions are generally taken in the political limelight, with
the political and media spotlight on the minister.

It must also be emphasised that some contacts take place at a
very high level within government, particularly when major companies are involved. For example, when ICI was worried about a
change in tax law which it thought would adversely affect its operations, meetings took place between the chairman of ICI and the
then Chancellor of the Exchequer, the Chief Secretary of the
Treasury, and other ministers and senior officials of the Inland
Revenue. It is not unknown for chairmen and managing directors
of major companies to have meetings at prime-ministerial level.

Policy implementation and enforcement

The consideration of policy implementation and enforcement really belongs to a discussion of relationships between pressure groups and the executive branch of government, even though Parliament has a role in the passage of delegated legislation. Many Acts of Parliament are largely put into effect through secondary legislation referred to as 'statutory instruments'. In particular, there has been a 'growth of Enabling Legislation, which outlines the parameters of a Statute's authority and delegates to Ministers the power to pass Regulations on specific matters within that authority' (Miller 1990, p. 58). Parliamentary scrutiny of such regulations is limited in its effect. Less than a quarter of the 2,500 or so statutory instruments made each year are referred to a Select Committee, 'whose duty is to scrutinize them under very restricted terms of reference' (Taylor 1979, p. 131).

Pressure groups are understandably very interested in the contents of statutory instruments. Detailed variations may influence considerably the activities and financial rewards of their members. Once again, there is an extensive process of consultation with potentially affected groups: for example, in the case of the Control of Pollution (Waste Disposal) Regulations 1987, eleven local-authority associations were consulted, plus fifty-two 'other interested bodies' ranging from Friends of the Earth to the British Insurance Brokers' Association (Norton 1990, p. 206). In dealing with delegated legislation, the executive reveals the extent of its reliance on the consent and expertise of pressure groups:

> Most instruments are only laid after consultation with affected interests. More so than primary legislation, delegated legislation is the product of negotiation within small policy communities of civil servants and affected groups. (In what has been termed quasi-legislation, notes of guidance and circulars drawn up under the authority of primary legislation, group representatives may perform the drafting.)
>
> (Norton 1990, p. 205)

Even when secondary legislation has been put into effect, and codes of conduct distributed, there is still a gap between implementation and enforcement. Passing a law offers the means of tackling a particular problem, but resources may not allow effective enforcement activity. Since the first anti-litter legislation was passed in Britain in the 1950s, the amount of litter on the streets has increased, and even the adoption of the problem as a 'crusade' by Mrs Thatcher had little visible impact. The enforcement of environmental legislation is often constrained by the limited staff resources available to the relevant inspectorate or other enforcing body. Many environmental groups consider that prosecutions are still not initiated in enough cases where environmental laws have been breached, although there is less reliance on persuading polluters to remedy their behaviour than in the past. In some cases, a pressure group is also responsible for enforcement, as in the case of the RSPCA and anti-cruelty laws:

> The biggest disadvantage for the RSPCA in its enforcement role is a lack of statutory power. Only the police have the power to arrest a person suspected of cruelty to animals and not even they . . . have the power to search the premises of a suspect since animal cruelty is not considered to be a serious enough offence . . . . This is not the case in America [where RSPCA equivalents] are incorporated as law-enforcement agencies.
>
> (Garner 1993, p. 189)

The benefits of being on the inside track

It is apparent from the evidence reviewed in this chapter that there are extensive contacts between pressure groups and the executive branches of government during the development of policy and its implementation. The growing importance of EU decisions, often highly technical in character, has increased the significance of such contacts. Many decisions are clearly taken within relatively closed policy communities in which the complexity of the problems being discussed often constitutes a significant entry barrier. Thus, in his discussion of food standards, Coates (1984, p. 157) observes the following:

> Possible changes are widely canvassed, thoroughly discussed, considered in detail and, if broadly acceptable to all who show an interest, put into effect . . . . This continuous process of consultation tends to commit the whole policy community not only to the policy process but also the decisions it brings forth . . . almost all members of the policy community have an interest in the smooth functioning of the system.

Consider the values that are embedded in that statement. The first is that of extensive and detailed consultation. The second is that of acceptability to affected interests. A third is the commitment of pressure groups to decisions arrived at through the process of consultation. A fourth is the assumption that both government and groups have an interest in continuity and stability in the policy process. These values might be summarised as the four Cs of insider pressure-group politics:

1. *consultation* with recognised interests
2. *consent* by the interest groups consulted to the decisions taken by government
3. *cooperation* by the groups in the implementation of the decisions
4. *continuity* in the contours of the policy-making process.

Such a policy process tends to benefit insider groups. Alternative channels are available to groups lacking insider status, through using the media to establish their concerns on the policy agenda, through the courts, or through the passage of private members' bills in Parliament. These methods will be considered in the next chapter. Miller (1990, pp. 53–6), from his vantage point as chief executive of Public Policy Consultants, assigns influence scores to various components of the political system. The prime minister receives a score of ten out of ten; officials eight; and ministers seven. Apart from the whips, the highest score given to a parliamentary body is six for back-bench (not select) committees of MPs and the House of Lords committee which scrutinises the activities of the EU. MPs/peers as a group receive four, rising to six if there is a small majority or a very public or political issue. Access to decision-makers in the executive branch clearly has its advantages.

4

Parliament

Parliament has conventionally been regarded as a route used to influence the decision-making process by outsider groups who lack good contacts with civil servants, but insider groups would appear to be even more active than outsider groups in terms of a range of different types of contact with Parliament. (Judge 1990a, p. 36). 'This suggests that, apart from their closer governmental links, insider groups are generally more active than outsider groups.' (Judge 1990a, p. 35) Although cause groups can sometimes attain their objectives through the passage of a private member's bill, sectional groups can also make effective use of parliamentary contacts. Bruce-Gardyne (1986, pp. 152–3) recalls what happened when, as a minister, he was presented with a complex scheme designed to enable horse traders to escape VAT:

> I was vastly unimpressed, until I was accosted by one of my senior colleagues in the corridors of Westminster. 'I hear', he told me in a voice full of menace, that 'you're being bloody-minded about our horse-trading scheme. Well forget it. It was all fixed up with your predecessor, and I can assure you that if you muck it around, we'll make your life a misery.' I had second thoughts.

For the greater part of the 1974–9 Parliament, the government lacked a majority, and this encouraged sectional groups to make greater use of contacts with Parliament to modify or overturn decisions. The CBI, for example, set up a parliamentary unit in 1977, developing a lobbying system based on that of the National Farmers' Union, with links at the constituency level between industrialists and their MPs. At Westminster, the CBI 'wooed the smallest parties' (MacDougall 1987, p. 232). The Scottish Nationalists were invited to CBI headquarters for a working dinner and 'were subsequently helpful on several occasions by casting their votes in the way we wanted' (p. 233). This period was significant not just because it brought about a lasting increase in the attention paid by sectional groups to Parliament, but also because it suggests that the importance of Parliament to pressure groups would be enhanced if a future government lacked an overall majority in the House of Commons.

Most associations representing particular industries will either have their own small staff dealing with Parliament, or retain a firm of parliamentary lobbyists to assist them with parliamentary representation. For example, the Chemical Industries Association (CIA) employs a parliamentary adviser, and administers the All Party Parliamentary Group for the Chemical Industry with a membership of some seventy MPs together with members of the House of Lords. The group meets to hear about developments in the industry and to discuss relevant legislation, and its members are also individually briefed on a large number of subjects. A piece of legislation which is particularly important to the CIA may involve the parliamentary adviser attending every debate and committee session in the Commons and Lords; briefing individual committee members, civil servants and ministers; and commenting on large numbers of amendments put down by MPs.

Ways of using Parliament

Parliament is made up of two houses; a variety of mechanisms for processing legislation and discussing current political issues; and (counting active peers) over a thousand individuals with a wide variety of political interests and priorities. How can pressure groups go about influencing a very complex institution which is understandably protective of its traditions and privileges?

One possibility is to organise a letter-writing campaign. Certainly, MPs are receiving more and more letters: one source has estimated that they were receiving twice as many letters in 1987 as they were seven years earlier (Public Policy Consultants 1987, p. 9). Many of these letters will, of course, be concerned with problems faced by individual constituents, and MPs will give consideration of such letters a high priority. Circulars from pressure groups are likely to receive little, if any, attention unless the MP or peer has a special interest in the issue. 'Perhaps half the mail sent to an MP is consigned to the bin by his secretary' (Miller 1990, p. 99).

One tactic that a pressure group may use to avoid the wastepaper basket is to get its members to write to their MP on an issue which concerns the group. Such a stratagem can backfire if it is not well managed. Bruce-Gardyne recalls that MPs received a larger number of letters in 1980 from Catholic constituents complaining about a plan to charge for school transport. 'On closer inspection most of these communications had fairly obviously been signed, not by Catholic voters at all, but by their children scribbling under the vigilant eye of their local parish priests' (Bruce-Gardyne 1986, p. 155). Far more effective was a lobby against new controls on shotgun ownership based on handwritten letters from the chairmen of village Conservative branches (p. 155).

MPs may be wined and dined to make them sympathetic to a particular point of view. Over two-thirds of those questioned by Public Policy Consultants thought that entertainment as a lobbying medium is over-used and under-exploited when it is used (Public Policy Consultants 1987, p. 25). All the ministers interviewed 'claimed that they would discount representations from MPs retained by organisations on whose behalf they were lobbying' (p. 27). Nevertheless, many organisations and companies – including, of course, trade unions – do retain MPs and peers.

What are they getting for their money, apart from the ability to dine important clients at Westminster, or to arrange meetings there (actually quite important motivations)? An MP or peer can, of course, put down a question as a means of obtaining information about government policy, although a pressure group with good civil service contacts should be able to obtain that anyway. However, in the case of oral questions it may sometimes be possible to embarrass the government into action through probing supplementaries. The MP or peer can raise matters through adjournment debates or, in the Lords, through the device of the Unstarred Question which leads to a debate. Early Day Motions (that is, motions that in practice are not debated) can be used to give publicity to a problem, although such motions have arguably been devalued through their over-use by professional lobbyists seeking to show their clients some tangible result for their fees. Nevertheless, they can be useful as a means of keeping a particular issue visible within the context of a broader campaign.

There is a particular danger of equating activity with effectiveness in the case of Parliament, and it should be remembered that it is very unusual for a government with a working majority to be defeated on the floor of the House of Commons on one of its bills. The government can make the matter one of confidence, as ultimately happened with the Maastricht treaty. Occasionally, of course, a government with a majority *may* be defeated on the floor of the House. This happened in April 1986 when a large-scale Conservative rebellion led to a government defeat on the Sunday trading bill at second reading stage. 'The various actors in the opposition were eventually directed in a well-run professional campaign in contrast to the lack-lustre and initially complacent campaign waged by the bill's supporters' (Bown 1990, p. 230). Such defeats are rare, however, and most of the rebellions which have been advertised in advance have ended up with the government suffering the embarrassment of a reduction in its majority, but with the legislation being passed intact.

A more successful strategy may be to change the detailed provisions of a bill in a way which is of benefit to a pressure group's members. An attempt can be made to do this at standing committee stage when the bill is considered line by line – although, of course, standing committees are whipped. There is, however, always the possibility of government back-benchers siding with the opposition to defeat a particular clause which concerns a pressure group. Sometimes they can be bought off with promises of future action, but from time to time the government considers that the best course of action is to make concessions. Thus, at standing committee stage 'The toing and froing between members and groups, either in person or through correspondence, is often continuous and extensive.' (Norton 1990, p. 186)

The House of Lords

Baldwin (1990, p. 158) argues that the House of Lords 'has increasingly become a focus for lobbying'. Perhaps the most important reason for this development has been the following:

growing assertiveness, making not merely drafting or technical
amendments to legislation but in changing it considerably. Between
1979 and 1987 the Conservative Government was defeated on 106
occasions . . . . The modern House of Lords is increasingly prepared
to create difficulties for the Government of the day. The fact that a
number of these defeats have forced the modification or withdrawal
of various proposals, as indeed have pressures from the peers which
did not lead to a defeat, has not gone unnoticed by pressure groups.
(Baldwin 1990, p. 159)

This growing assertiveness can in part be seen as a response to
what often seemed to be the weaknesses of the opposition in the
House of Commons, particularly up to 1992. It has been relatively
easy for the House of Lords to assert that it is the voice of the
people, or of disadvantaged groups, when it is facing what has
often been a very unpopular Conservative government. (Its critics
would claim it is the last refuge of the old establishment displaced
by Thatcherism.) It would, however, be more difficult for the
Lords to assert itself against a new Labour government, particularly if reform of the upper house was under consideration.

Nevertheless, the House of Lords offers another opportunity to
make detailed amendments. If they are too contentious, they are
likely to be reversed when the measure returns to the Commons.
However, the House of Lords offers fruitful ground for inserting
relatively technical amendments which may be important to a pressure group's members. Even if the amendment is not pressed to a
vote, it may be used to extract further assurances from the government. This is a tactic which has been used with considerable success
by the CBI over the years. When the 1966–70 Labour Government
announced its intention to reform the Lords, the CBI stated that it
would 'take any opportunity of advocating the retention of arrangements which would preserve the advantages industry has enjoyed
under the present system' (CBI Annual Report 1967, p. 22). Indeed,
Bruce-Gardyne (1986, p. 147) argues that 'Whitehall remains ill-
equipped to handle the House of Lords'. It is not easy to find able
junior ministers to represent a department in the Lords, and they
are then called upon to handle all aspects of its work.

Private bills

Private bills (not private *members'* bills) constitute a form of legislation which is often of particular interest to sectional pressure

groups. Without going into all the complexities of this particular type of legislation (there are also hybrid bills), these are largely bills promoted by local authorities or nationalised industries to acquire land or undertake some new activity. In 1994, a private bill brought forward by British Rail to construct a new railway across London (Cross Rail) was defeated in committee. Proposals put forward by Labour-controlled local authorities have sometimes attracted the opposition of bodies such as the CBI. As many as seventy bills of this type may be passed in a parliamentary session, with much of the work being undertaken in the Lords. The committee stage of such bills has a quasi-judicial character, with counsel representing both sides and evidence given on oath. Because of the expense involved, promoters of such measures are generally willing to enter into discussions before committee stage to agree amendments. They are sometimes the subject of intensive lobbying. P & O encountered controversy 'after they hosted a party in the House of Commons at the same time a Private Bill they were sponsoring to extend Felixstowe docks was being discussed on the floor of the House'

(Grantham and Seymour-Ure 1990, p. 75)

Parliamentary committees

Executive policies and actions are scrutinised by select committees of both Houses. Pressure groups dutifully prepare memoranda of evidence for such bodies, and the more important ones are asked to present themselves to answer questions from committee members:

> Outside interests . . . make a substantial input to the evidence received by select committees and in written evidence make the largest contribution to all except four committees . . . [pressure groups] . . . are a major source for committees of non-governmental information.
>
> (Rush 1990, p. 145)

In selecting subjects for investigation, select committees invariably bear in mind the amount of media interest that a particular investigation may attract. Thus, in the 1993–4 session, investigations into the Child Support Agency by the Social Security Committee attracted considerable attention, given that the subject of its activities was the focus of extensive public debate. Other investigations may be followed closely in specialised policy communities. For example, the investigation by the House of Commons Agriculture Committee in the 1994–5 session into the difficulties encountered in reforming the milk marketing scheme, with evidence given by the NFU and the Dairy Trade Federation, was followed closely in the specialist farming press and by members of the agricultural policy community.

Bruce-Gardyne represents the dismissive executive view of select committees when he states that they 'produce a constant flow of reports which are rarely discussed in Parliament, and seldom make a stir . . . rarely, in practice, do they make much impact on departmental policies' (1986, p. 141). Members of the Study of Parliament Group, on the other hand, tend to take a positive view when looking at the role of select committees from the perspective of legislative studies specialists. Thus, Rush argues (1990, p. 148):

> In so far as select committees can make recommendations, a significant proportion of which are accepted by the government, it is likely that pressure groups do have some effect from time to time. One of the attractions of select committees for outside interests is that they generally operate in a less partisan atmosphere than other areas of Commons activity . . . . Many of the recommendations made in committee reports concern the details of policy, rather than the principle, and the details of policy are what many outside organizations are interested in influencing.

Of course, even if government accepts recommendations in a select committee report, it may be because government thinking was moving in that direction anyway, and the committee has absorbed some of the drift of thinking from civil servants who have given evidence. One would also need to ask whether the recommendations, once accepted, were actually implemented in an effective way. The Public Accounts Committee is the committee that has been most effective in following through earlier investigations, but then it has the resources of the National Audit Office at its disposal.

Peter Riddell, the political editor of *The Times*, has argued that it is the hearings rather than the reports that matter. Extracts are shown on television each morning and are watched by those with a serious interest in politics, such as political correspondents (seminar by Peter Riddell, Oxford, May 1994). There is no doubt that the reputations of ministers and others can be diminished by poor performances. For example, it was claimed that Clare Spottis-woode, the new head of Ofgas, had not helped her standing by a disappointing performance in front of the Energy Committee. However, pressure groups are more interested in policies than personalities and political careers. While acknowledging their increasing expertise and useful scrutiny of public bodies, Miller lists their weaknesses as 'Executive may ignore their work' and 'Usually work too late to influence policy' (Miller 1990, p. 55).

In practice, some of the most influential bodies in Parliament are the little-known but important specialist back-bench committees of MPs interested in a particular subject. Clearly, it is the back-bench committees of the governing party that are of real importance; such committees happen to be better developed in the Conservative Party. Miller (p. 40) notes that particularly 'At a time of large Government majorities they are a powerful focus for back-bench opinion on the Government side, with privileged access to Ministers and a representative role enhanced by their regular meetings, at which business, industry and other interest groups are given the opportunity to voice their concerns or be questioned by MPs.' Even with a much smaller majority after 1992, the factionalised and restive state of the Conservative Party meant that ministers had to be attentive to back-bench opinion, recalling the adage that 'your opponents are in front of you, but your enemies are behind you' in the Commons.

Ministers have been persuaded to drop contentious proposals because of a back-bench revolt in one of these committees, as happened, for example, with the Thatcher Government's first set of proposals to introduce student loans. Lawson recalls that among the bodies he consulted in the Conservative Party while drafting the Budget were the executive committee of the 1922 Committee and the back-bench Finance Committee, with the whole Treasury team going to the latter meeting. 'On occasion, they could influence events: for example, the introduction of cash accounting for VAT for small businesses in my 1987 Budget . . . stemmed directly from views expressed at these meetings.' (Lawson 1992, p. 320) The back-bench specialist committees are therefore an important target for pressure-group activity at Westminster. They have, however, tended to be weaker in the Labour Party and might be less significant in a future Labour government than they have been under the Conservatives since 1979.

Professional lobbyists

There has been increasing concern about the ethical issues raised by the proliferation of professional 'lobbyists' offering to act as intermediaries between pressure groups and Parliament (or, for that matter, Whitehall, although Parliament is often their main field of activity). As Grantham and Seymour-Ure (1990, p. 78) comment:

> Questions about whether a lobbying approach is quite what it seems bump up against the traditional interest-group problem of the boundaries of legitimate behaviour . . . . In particular, how does one balance protection from improper pressure with citizens' right to make representations to their Members?

Sectional groups and companies are the main users of the services of professional lobbyists, although well-resourced cause groups may have their own parliamentary lobbyist. Much of the work of lobbyists often consists of monitoring developments, and drawing the attention of clients to emerging issues which should concern them. Given that they have staff reading *Hansard* and other parliamentary documents for a number of clients, they are often able to provide such a service more economically than if a pressure group tried to undertake this sifting work for itself. They also build up a body of knowledge about the special interests of MPs, which they can utilise to meet the particular needs of their clients. One consultant explained in interview that the nature of the work

> depends on the nature of the lobby, depends on what one's objectives are. There are 101 different things – identifying MPs who are personally interested and sympathetic, briefing people before Second Readings in public bills, suggesting amendments, a lot of work during standing committees.

Some of the most difficult ethical questions in this area relate to those MPs who are directly involved in the running of such companies, estimated to be thirty-six in 1989 (Grantham and Seymour-Ure 1990, p. 68). There is concern about whether customers might gain the impression that it was possible to buy access, given that the fees of these professional lobbyists are not low. Concern has been expressed that 'the better organised and richer interests will push out the less so' (Doig 1986, p. 43). Claims of this kind were made in 1994 when it was alleged that a lobbying firm 'played a key role in securing the blocking of [a] private member's Bill banning tobacco advertising' (The *Independent*, 14 May 1994).

However, it must be noted that, although many consultancy firms are very politically sophisticated and display a high level of professional skill, there is always an element of the 'emperor's clothes' about the work of professional lobbyists. There is never a tangible end-product which can be attributed to the efforts of the lobbyist; if the campaign is successful, it may have nothing to do with the lobbyist's efforts. Some less-informed clients are too easily impressed by having lunches arranged with MPs, or with being escorted to meetings at the Palace of Westminster. Even so, 'there are various cases which suggest that consultants have achieved for clients outcomes that otherwise were unlikely to have been achieved' (Grantham and Seymour-Ure 1990, p. 73).

One of the reasons why MPs are sometimes receptive to professional lobbyists is that they are overworked and poorly provided with support staff and facilities. Improvements in this area might help to offset worries about the susceptibility of MPs to external pressures. Even so, as the House of Commons Select Committee on Members' Interests stated in one of its reports on the issue, 'It is the right of any citizen to lobby his Member of Parliament, and if he considers that his case can be better advanced with professional assistance he has every right to avail himself of that assistance' (House of Commons 1985, p. iii).

The issue of regulating the conduct of lobbyists is unlikely to go away, if only because it is a popular subject for television producers. Some of the media exposés are rather sensationalist and try to build a general argument from particular instances. However, if nothing is done, the standing both of Parliament and of the many reputable firms operating in this area, could be seriously damaged. The argument against compulsory registration is that it would give those registered a kind of official standing.

Five of the leading lobbying firms, with a turnover of at least £10 million between them, are proposing to set up an Association of Political Consultants as a substitute for regulation by Parliament (which would be their preference). The body would propose a code of professional ethics and would be responsible for disciplining its members should the code of practice be breached. It would also maintain a voluntary register of professional lobbyists (*Financial Times*, 23 February 1994).

Private members' bills

Private members' bills offer one route by which pressure groups, particularly cause groups, can hope to attain their objectives. However, it is a hazardous route, even for relatively uncontentious proposals, and has probably become more so as opponents of such bills have made more use of consulting firms to advise on blocking tactics. Relatively few private members' measures ever become law:

> The scales are heavily weighted against them. In the first place the Government takes up most of the time of the House for its own business, so that a Private Member has to be more than fortunate to get enough time to take a Bill through all its stages before the end of the Session. In the second place it is difficult for a Private Member to organize a majority favourable towards his Bill – or, as is more usually the case, to prevent a majority of unfavourable Members voting against it.
>
> (Taylor 1979, p. 89)

Capital punishment was abolished, abortion legalised, divorce liberalised and theatre censorship ended through private members' legislation, but the period between 1964 and 1970 was exceptional. Major changes were brought about through private members' legislation during this period 'because the Labour Government granted time to the various bills' (Marsh and Read 1988, p. 64). Far more typical of the successful use of private members' legislation by pressure groups is the relatively technical measure which offends no important countervailing interest. A member who wins a high place on the ballot for private members' bills will receive many approaches from groups who would like said member to introduce their proposals as bills. Marsh and Read (pp. 63–4) cite the case of a Conservative MP who, having specified 'no animals, no sex', was offered a bill by the British Insurance Brokers' Association who wanted to establish a register for legitimate insurance brokers. 'The bill was passed without a vote although there was considerable debate and the Government granted time for the consideration of Lords amendments' (p. 64).

Abortion is one of the most emotive issues in contemporary politics, and bills designed to restrict the liberalisation introduced by the 1967 Act have become a recurrent feature of the parliamentary calendar. However, it is difficult to dislodge private members' legislation once it has been passed, and it is therefore important to consider briefly how the original legislation reached the statute book. Founded in 1936, the Abortion Law Reform Association (ALRA) was regarded for many years as 'a morally subversive, crank organisation' (Hindell and Simms 1974, p. 162). In 1963 ALRA leadership positions were taken over by a new group of younger leaders dissatisfied with the organisation's level of effectiveness. A number of factors contributed to the success of the Steel bill, including the presence of a new wave of liberally minded MPs elected in 1964 and 1966, and what amounted to government support for reform (see Marsh and Chambers 1981, pp. 17–21). Public opinion was, however, undoubtedly an important factor:

> The abortion lobby became successful when it was able to demonstrate to Parliament that despite religious opposition, public opinion had finally caught up with the views it had been expressing for thirty years. The lobby did not create this opinion, for many factors were at work, but it did influence public opinion, hasten it, and organize it when the time was ripe.
>
> (Hindell and Simms 1974, p. 163)

The anti-abortion lobby has grown considerably in strength since 1967 (the first anti-abortion group was launched during the passage of the Steel bill), but it has not been successful in repealing, or substantially amending, the 1967 legislation. Defenders of the status quo have the advantage that they can use parliamentary procedure to help to defeat attempts at change. Despite the strength of the anti-abortion lobbies at constituency level, 'It was inside Parliament that the battle was really won by the strategy, effort and organization of the pro-abortion lobby' (Marsh and Chambers 1981, p. 163). The failure of the Corrie Bill which sought to amend radically the 1967 Act 'shows how important a knowledge of parliamentary procedure is for parliamentary interest groups. The pro-abortion side was better versed in procedure, and on most occasions better at using it' (p. 191). Although both sides had very effective whipping systems to mobilise their supporters, the pro-abortion lobby was better organised (Marsh and Read 1988, p. 130).

Although the legalisation of abortion was influenced by evidence about the state of public opinion, having public opinion on your side is not sufficient to ensure the passage of a private member's bill. Polls conducted since the late 1950s have shown that a growing majority of the population favour the abolition of hunting. Over the 1970s and 1980s polls 'showed a hardening of opinion against fox hunting . . . and by the early 1980s some polls were indicating 80 per cent support for a ban' (Garner 1993, p. 47). Attempts to ban blood sports through private members' legislation have, however, failed. This was partly because of the political skills of a group of pro-hunting Conservative MPs, and partly because of the 'vagaries of the procedures for Private Members' bills in the House of Commons' (Thomas 1983, p. 268). In addition, 'Blood sports enthusiasts have increasingly (and cleverly) turned their attention to conservation justifications' (Garner 1993, p. 173).

The League Against Cruel Sports decided that, rather than trying to pursue the fruitless route of private members' legislation, it would be better to use evidence of public opinion to persuade the Labour Party to adopt a manifesto commitment to abolish hunting. It was argued that 'only a government bill would succeed in passing all the parliamentary stages and only a manifesto commitment would be likely to get sufficient parliamentary time and attention to get the bill through the Lords' (Thomas 1983, p. 222). This decision represents a significant recognition of the limitations of private members' bills as a means for cause groups to attain their objectives. The Labour Party manifesto commitment was diluted between 1983 and 1992 (Garner 1993, pp. 201–2). Even if it is included in the next Labour manifesto, questions would remain about how high a priority such legislation would be given relative to other policy changes a Labour government would want to introduce.

Conclusions

As Parliament has appeared to become a more independent and authoritative body, pressure groups have given a higher priority to influencing it. This can also reflect a frustration with other channels, so that for industrialists under the Thatcher Government, 'increased attention to parliament was a reflection of manufacturing industry's general belief that its sectoral voices no longer carried the same resonance in Whitehall and a . . . desire to develop supplementary channels through which these voices could be amplified.' (Judge 1990b, p. 221). The increased activity of parliamentary consultants has also had a supply side-effect in terms of the creation of a market for their advice.

The reappearance of a 'hung Parliament' in the future would enhance the importance of Parliament in the decision-making process and to pressure groups. Under more normal conditions, however, the executive remains the arena in which pressure can usually most effectively be applied, before the government has closed its options and publicly committed itself to a particular course of action. Governments can be forced to back down, but it is not easy, and it doesn't happen very often. 'Ultimately, the point of pressure of party committees, all-party groups, and consultants and their clients alike is the executive.' (Judge 1990b, p. 222). An effective pressure group must pay attention to Parliament, but it is unlikely to be its main channel of access to decision-makers.

5

Exerting pressure outside Whitehall and Westminster

Although much pressure-group activity is directed towards the executive and Parliament, many important activities take place outside Whitehall and Westminster. Pressure groups are potential competitors with political parties for members and influence, and this chapter reviews the nature of the relationship between the two. As the mass media have established a more central role in the political process, as older political structures have declined in importance, securing media attention has become a central pressure-group activity. Some pressure groups are making increasing use of the courts as a means of securing their objectives. Changes in local government towards a greater emphasis on partnership relationships are opening up new opportunities for pressure groups to participate in policy formation and implementation.

Pressure groups and the party system

In approaching ministers and MPs, pressure groups are dealing with members of political parties. Sometimes, party channels may be a useful means of bringing pressure to bear on a minister, as was noted in the discussion of the specialist back-bench committees within the parliamentary parties. The focus in this section, however, is on influencing the political parties outside Parliament. As was noted in Chapter 1, there are some pressure groups that exist solely within political parties with the object of influencing their policies, but the discussion here will be concerned with pressure groups which use contacts with the political parties as a means of attaining their objectives.

There is a sense in which political parties and pressure groups are competitors: for members, for activists, and for influence. As political-party membership has declined, pressure-group membership has grown. Of course, it is not a case of an either/or choice between the two. Seyd and Whiteley's large-scale study of Labour Party members shows that 16 per cent of those surveyed were also members of Greenpeace, 8.2 per cent were members of Friends of the Earth and 6.8 per cent were members of Amnesty International (Seyd and Whiteley 1992, p. 92).

Even so, there is probably some causal connection between the decline of party membership and the rise of a new generation of pressure groups. Individuals who have found the existing political parties too formal, hidebound and slow to attain results may have opted for the fresher and more innovative political policies and strategies being pursued by pressure groups. As Porritt and Winner (1988, p. 69) note, 'it is precisely the inability of the Labour Party to dig itself out of its own fossilized form of in-fighting which understandably makes Greens doubt that they are likely to embrace green politics at anything more than the most superficial level'. For a young person, sitting in a tree to oppose a new by-pass is likely to seem both more exciting and more directly effective than getting a resolution passed on road-building at the Labour Party branch meeting to be forwarded to the annual conference.

The relationship between pressure groups and political parties has been one of the less-developed aspects of the literature, but a significant new contribution has been made by Robinson (1992). He notes (p. 4) that 'The conventional interpretation used to explain why the political parties respond to the environmental movement has centred upon a "pressure-response" mechanism'. An alternative model 'deliberately excludes external inputs and the lines of contact extend only within the boundaries of party, to emphasise how a party can "green" itself' (p. 125). This 'intentional' model embodies such factors as party ideology, party policy, a receptive climate to green ideas, mediated through 'genuine concerns' and 'strategic considerations' to explain the process of 'party greening' (p. 125).

While acknowledging the contribution of this latter model in explaining the extent of party 'greening' in the 1980s, an analysis of pressure groups is necessarily going to focus on the 'pressure-response' model. Here, Robinson shows how the Green Alliance has harnessed the competition for voters between the political parties. 'With a staff of only four in 1988 and a relatively small but prestigious membership (approximately 450 in 1988) of key environmentalists and personalities, the Green Alliance has cultivated insider status within the major parties.' (p. 96) An insider strategy directed at the parties rather than the executive is a novel one. Although its success may be influenced by the electorate's apparent level of concern with environmental issues at any given time, the sophistication with which it has been executed appears to have paid dividends (p. 97):

> The subtlety of such pressure politics seems to have found favour with politicians, who appreciate the sensitivity and political understanding shown . . . the Green Alliance was seen as instrumental in ensuring that all parties included detailed statements on the environment in their manifestos, leading up to the 1987 election.

It should also be noted that political parties may wish to use pressure groups as allies, particularly in the mobilisation of support. Thus, for example, when water privatisation legislation was introduced into Parliament in 1988, Labour's spokesperson on the issue announced her intention 'to enlist the help of outside pressure groups, such as Greenpeace and Friends of the Earth, to help press home the environmental protection case to the voters' (*Financial Times*, 7 December 1988). Similarly, in the 1970s the Conservatives set up a Private Enterprise Consultative Council, with eighteen trade associations as founder members, serviced by their Small Business Bureau. 'There is no doubt that it served the party's electoral interests to sympathize with, to encourage, small business organizations and to attempt to incorporate them' (Elliott *et al.* 1982, p. 83). Parties may also, however, be concerned with strengthening pressure groups to assist policy implementation. Worried about the lack of CBI influence over pay negotiations – a problem which would become more serious if an attempt were made to pursue a full-employment policy – a group of social scientists close to the Labour

Party discussed ways of improving the CBI's organisational strength in the run-up to the 1987 general election.

One of the main strategies used by pressure groups in relation to political parties is to seek to persuade them to adopt resolutions which will lead to a manifesto commitment to adopt the group's objectives. Such an approach is particularly relevant in relation to the Labour Party where the party conference has a greater formal role in making policy than in the Conservative Party, although in some ways recently it has become managed more as a presentational event at the same time as the Conservative conference has become less docile. The Conservative Party does not offer the same opportunities for exerting influence on a clearly defined and relatively democratic process for deciding party policy.

Nevertheless, lobbyists turn up in large numbers at the Conservative as well as at the Labour annual conference (the parties make money out of letting them set up stalls) and at the smaller party conferences as well, if only to keep in touch with the pulse of party opinion, and perhaps to seize the chance for a discreet word with a minister. 'Although cosmetic on one level, decisions to invest thousands of pounds in exhibition stands, or to host receptions and fringe meetings, are not taken lightly' (Berry 1992, p. 228). Berry notes (p. 228) that a fringe meeting at the 1991 Conservative Conference organised by a lobbying firm on behalf of a number of regiments served the purpose of emphasising Conservative grass-roots opposition to regimental amalgamations.

In general, however, links between pressure groups and political parties are not well developed. Except in special cases such as the anti-hunting lobby, developing overly close links with one political party would be counterproductive, as it would mean that the group would be influential only when that party was in power and might not be very influential even then because its support would be taken for granted. As pointed out in Chapter 1, pressure groups and political parties are essentially different political formations. Political parties wish to win office, in part to put a political programme into effect, but also to keep out the opposing party, and to give their leaders the opportunity of ministerial office. Pressure groups are not seeking office, and their objectives are highly specific rather than broadly based programmes; indeed, in many cases, they are seeking to ameliorate difficulties caused for their members as a result of the implementation of party programmes.

Pressure groups and the media

The media play a crucial role in modern politics. As one former Cabinet minister has noted, 'The Cabinet increasingly, as the years go on, tends to be most concerned with the agenda that the press and media are setting out as the crucial issues before the nation at any time' (Boyle 1971, p. 109). It is therefore not surprising that the effective management of relations with the media has become a crucial skill for pressure groups.

The term 'media' covers a variety of forms of dissemination – television, radio, the press, etc. – and, within each of those forms, material that is targeted at a variety of audiences. Television thus carries mass-audience programmes and also programmes likely to be watched by a very small audience interested in a particular issue. The press ranges from mass-circulation tabloids, through quality newspapers, to highly specialised journals and magazines. Reviewing the ways in which environmental issues are placed on the political agenda, Robinson observes (1992, p. 110):

> Specialist programmes such as BBC 2's 'Nature' provide analysis on the full range of environmental issues, whilst the investigative television journalism of programmes such as 'Panorama', 'World in Action' and 'First Tuesday' has increasingly been used to 'expose' national and international environmental problems . . . . Following the broadcast of such programmes, MPs can find themselves under pressure from an enquiring public with regard to issues they had previously given little consideration.

Sometimes it will be advantageous for pressure groups to try and reach the largest possible audience through a medium such as the television news or a mass-circulation newspaper. On other occasions, however, a more targeted approach may be desirable. It may be more appropriate to aim to influence informed opinion through the quality newspapers which are read by large numbers of decision-makers. Current-affairs radio programmes have a significant audience among politicians, who are said to compete with each other to get on the *Today* programme broadcast in the mornings on Radio 4, which can help to set the day's political agenda.

Each policy community will also tend to support its own specialist press. For example, in the case of agriculture, there are special radio programmes for farmers; broadsheets such as the *Financial Times* have agricultural correspondents (often working farmers);

there are general publications such as *Farmers' Weekly* which often interview senior politicians on agricultural issues – the Prime Minister in May 1994; an expensive but high-quality newsletter on EU developments, *Agra Europe*; and even more specialist publications, such as *The Sheep Farmer*, dealing with particular branches of agriculture. Some idea of the scale of the specialist press in agriculture is given by the fact that the Guild of Agricultural Journalists has 520 members.

Important interventions may come from unexpected sections of the media. Marsh and Chambers note that the Corrie abortion bill was attacked by the whole range of women's magazines. Most surprising was the 'strong attack on the Bill which came from *Woman's Own*, a magazine not known for its radical views and with a largely conservative readership' (Marsh and Chambers 1981, p. 133). Indeed, *Woman's Own* paid for an opinion poll which provided evidence of widespread public opposition to the Corrie bill and was sent by the magazine to all MPs just before the debate at report stage. One MP listed it as one of the reasons why the bill eventually failed (p. 146). More generally, 'The women's magazines carried the pro-abortion lobby's message far more widely than ever before, and not just to the more radical women. The anti-abortion groups lacked this kind of publicity' (p. 133).

One indication of the increased importance of the media is the greater attention they have been given from the 1970s onwards by established insider groups. Groups which in the past had relied largely on behind-the-scenes contacts in Whitehall found that such a strategy was no longer adequate; it was also necessary to try and create a favourable public image to reinforce their contacts with civil servants and politicians. For example, in 1977 the CBI initiated an annual conference, a move which it described as 'the CBI "goes public" for the first time' (CBI Annual Report 1977, p. 10).

It is not just sectional groups that have been giving a greater priority to media relations. Established cause groups have also revised their strategies to give a new emphasis to contacts with the press. For example, the Council for the Protection of Rural England (CPRE) was run for nearly forty years by a general secretary whose 'style of operation was through personal contact in the corridors of power. He fastidiously avoided embarrassing those whom he influenced or sought to influence' (Lowe and Goyder 1983, p. 75). The CPRE subsequently became more media conscious, with an increasingly sophisticated approach to the use of the media. Thus, when a new director was appointed in 1980, he 'had experience in advertising and freelance writing for television and radio' (p. 75).

How pressure groups use the media

Contacts with the media are clearly important to a wide range of pressure groups. However, in what particular ways do pressure groups use the media? It is suggested that six distinct uses can be identified: visibility, information, climate, reactive response, influence and content.

Visibility refers to the use of the media to establish a presence, and to recruit and retain members. The Aberdeen group's data show that of the members of Friends of the Earth surveyed 23.6 per cent joined after seeing a press/media campaign. The groups are commercial clients of the press, as well as providers of news:

> Greenpeace, for example, is regularly contacted by newspapers alerting them to advertising possibilities when an environmental story is being published. Thus, on a page with a lead story and a picture of environmental damage or stricken wildlife, the group will have a membership advertisement.
> (Jordan, Maloney and McLaughlin 1994b, p. 551)

The sinking of the Braer oil tanker off the Shetlands in 1993 provoked a wave of group advertising, and by joining or sending money to the group concerned, readers could feel that they were doing something to help the afflicted animals and birds. Some publicity comes free, however, and is not linked to a disaster. For example, a television programme called *The Animals Film* 'was an important moment in the growth of public awareness of animal exploitation' (Porritt and Winner 1988, p. 52). The animal protection movement has found that the media are more interested in wild animals, particularly endangered species, but this may be changing (Garner 1993, p. 65). It may also be that television audiences feel more comfortable identifying with, say, pandas in China than with farm animals in Europe. Retaining members is a problem for many cause groups and constant exposure for the group in the media reassures its membership that it is active, and helps in the retention of members. There is little point in recruiting a large number of new members as a result of a blitz of media activity if their interest cannot be engaged and their support retained.

The media can be an important source of *information* for pressure groups. The trade press can unwittingly reveal clues about what a particular firm or industry is doing. 'Lobbyists scan the papers in the search for stories, data, opinions and letters related to themselves' (Davies 1985, p. 181). Frank Field recalls how the Child Poverty Action Group (CPAG) carefully read the court page to produce a list of individuals who had access to the then prime minister (Field 1982, p. 54).

Climate refers to the long-term efforts of pressure groups to change the climate of opinion on an issue in a way that is favourable to their objectives. This may involve seeking to influence informed opinion and decision-makers, but it is also important to seek long-run changes in public values which set the context within which policy is made. 'Through their background campaigns, environmental groups in general have enhanced their public image and generated a climate of opinion sympathetic to environmental protection' (Lowe and Goyder 1983, p. 79).

Reactive response is necessary when a news story emerges that is relevant to a group's concerns or activities. Sometimes an organisation may have to react very quickly to an unfavourable story: for example, the egg industry was obliged to react in December 1988 to a statement by a junior minister, Edwina Currie, about allegedly extensive contamination of eggs by salmonella. In such circumstances, a group may be forced into a defensive stance. However, properly managed, such situations can be used to create favourable publicity, particularly for cause groups. The group may be invited on a television programme to explain its position, or can at least write to the press in response to editorials or letters from others.

Using the media as a means of exerting *influence* on government is clearly particularly important. Of course, ministers are not usually going to change their policies because of a newspaper editorial or a critical television programme, but the sudden development of a campaign in the media may catch them off guard and oblige them to respond. Media coverage can reinforce a case being made to civil servants by demonstrating that the matter is one of public concern. It may help to move the problem up the political agenda. Field recalls that one way of getting the CPAG's correspondence 'onto the top of the pile and read by ministers was to ensure publicity for the letters in the media . . . ministers would then request an internal briefing, thereby getting the department's attention onto the issue being raised by the Group' (Field 1982, pp. 53–4). Lowe and Goyder show how environmental groups have been able to use media coverage to arouse public opinion and obtain a response from a previously indifferent government department. In relation to issues such as the introduction of lead-free petrol and against the introduction of heavier lorries, 'the intense media interest transformed what had previously been a humdrum administrative matter into a sensitive political issue' (Lowe and Goyder 1983, p. 79).

Publicity to exert influence requires a rather different strategy, however, from that used by a group seeking visibility to get established. At that stage, a variety of stunts may be a justifiable means of launching the group and attracting members. However, Whiteley and Winyard's research (1987, p. 130) makes it clear that groups can be damaged by irresponsible publicity. Civil servants do not like groups who appear to be more interested in television publicity than in serious negotiations. Explaining the difference between responsible and irresponsible publicity, Whiteley and Winyard (p. 120) comment:

> Responsible publicity meant coverage in the quality press about the group's activities and the needs of its clients. Primarily it involved a reasoned presentation of the group's case. It did not involve attacks on the character and motives of ministers and officials, or illegal demonstrations such as sit-ins in supplementary benefits offices. These were seen as counterproductive.

Finally, pressure groups may lobby the media directly and attempt to influence the *content* of its output. Various pressure groups have been concerned about scripts used on the radio series *The Archers*. The programme's producers 'are heavily lobbied by all and sundry' (quoted in Porritt and Winner 1988, p. 127). When one of the younger characters caught the green bug and started investigating the use of bovine somatotrophin on dairy herds, complaints were received from the farming establishment. When one of the characters, Susan Carter, was sent to prison, a 'Free the Ambridge One' campaign led to a debate about sentencing policy and a statement from the Home Secretary.

Whiteley and Winyard (1987, p. 10) note that a number of changes in the political environment have produced a situation in which 'Ministers and officials who might have reacted with hostility to the publicity associated with lobbying activity in the 1980s now regard it as a more normal aspect of campaign strategy.' Certainly, media coverage is generally an asset for cause groups, whereas sectional groups are often obliged to give it a greater emphasis as a defensive response. However, it is also important to remember the limits of media publicity. It is essentially ephemeral in character (this is particularly true of television); the media's attention span on an issue is necessarily limited; and politicians may be able to stall on an issue until attention has shifted elsewhere. As Porritt and Winner (1988, p. 86) comment, 'If a nation's ecological wisdom were measured by the number of television programmes it makes about the environment, Britain would have little to worry about.'

Obtaining media publicity can become a substitute for effective political action that actually changes policy outcomes. Greenpeace has been criticised for engaging in media stunts which may then mislead supporters into thinking that policy has been changed:

> For example, watching a handful of heroic Greenpeace 'rainbow warriors' . . . on television, the audience may think that effective action has already taken place . . . . Coping with the many persistent environmental problems . . . requires a steadier engagement at the international level, and changes in personal behaviour, instead of merely spectacular, predominantly symbolic, actions which may simply soothe the broader public.
>
> (Rucht 1993, p. 93)

Media coverage is a means of changing the political agenda, but it is important not to underestimate the forces which produce continuity in political decision-making.

Pressure groups and the courts

Pressure groups make less use of the courts in Britain than they do in the United States, but more use than they did, say, twenty years ago. There are a number of reasons why American pressure groups make more use of the courts – not least because the United States is a more litigious society, with a high number of lawyers per head of population – but the litigious habit is spreading to Britain.

The American legal system takes a more generous view of what constitutes 'legal standing' than is the case in Britain. 'In sum, US law erects the lowest entry barriers against both associations and individuals wishing to challenge administrative decisions in court' (Brickman *et al.* 1985, p. 110). Thus, public-interest associations that would be restricted from taking legal action in Britain 'can sue with relative ease in the United States pursuant to specific statutes and judicially defined standing rules' (p. 126).

Legal actions are costly and can take a long time to complete. Even if a group wins a victory in litigation, government may reverse the decision in subsequent legislation. It is therefore not surprising that Whiteley and Winyard (1987, p. 108) found that the great majority of groups in their sample 'have not seen the judicial process as a significant focus of their activities in attempting to influence policy making'. Test cases were mainly seen as a means of influencing the implementation stage of the policy process. They can sometimes be useful 'as an opportunity to politicize an issue and to exert pressure for changes in the law' (p. 108).

There may be cases where pressure groups resort to the courts when other strategies have failed. Following the defeat of the Corrie bill, the anti-abortion lobby switched its attention away from attempts to amend the 1967 Act in Parliament. As one alternative, they used the courts 'to attempt to establish a body of case law which would ensure that doctors were more circumspect and therefore less liberal in their interpretation of the Abortion Act' (Marsh and Read 1988, p. 132).

A particularly significant court challenge was that brought by Greenpeace (along with Lancashire County Council) in an attempt to prevent British Nuclear Fuels (BNF) opening and commissioning its £2.8 billion Thorp reprocessing plant. Although Greenpeace lost the case in the High Court, they did not have to pay BNF's legal expenses and the judge ruled that 'government lawyers had "erred in law" when they argued that ministers were not legally bound to justify the need for Thorp' and 'emphasised the need "to properly inform the public" on matters such as Thorp' *(Financial Times,* 5/6 March 1994).

The political parties, particularly Labour, were ambivalent about Thorp, which employs 2,000 in a region of high unemployment, and is supported by the constituency MP, Jack Cunningham, the shadow foreign secretary in 1994:

In contrast Whitehall officials credit the pressure groups with having forced the government to re-examine Thorp's future, even if they did not eventually change its mind. Part of that influence, officials make clear, was the pressure groups' increasing use of the courts. Officials say Greenpeace's threat of legal action . . . prompted a second public consultation into the plant, delaying the go-ahead by several months.

(Maddox 1994, p. 8)

Whether securing a delay was worth the effort, and the cost if Greenpeace had had to contribute to the government's legal costs, is a matter of opinion. Within Greenpeace, there was certainly concern that the group might be moving away from its supporters' priorities which could be whales and toxic wastes rather than nuclear power. The campaigns director of Friends of the Earth announced, however, that they would be 'stepping up lawsuits against the government and companies . . . "European regulation has given us a particularly good lever"' (Maddox 1994, p. 8). As an example of more successful court action, when the Conservative Government published its plans for privatising the water industry, it originally intended to transfer the regulatory function to the private sector with the rest of the industry. The Government subsequently backed down in the face of a legal challenge based on European law made by the CPRE and the Institute for European Environmental Policy (Richardson, Maloney and Rüdig 1992, p. 164).

The law can also be used against pressure groups. Lynx, the radical anti-fur campaign, lost a libel case brought by a mink farm and was ordered to pay £40,000 damages plus costs which, with its own costs, produced a total bill of £260,000. Lynx went into liquidation and two of its staff were declared bankrupt. The libel case constrained Lynx's activities for a two-year period. A successor organisation, Respect for Animals, was established in December 1993.

Local government

The 1980s saw a significant reduction in the independence and powers of local government in Britain through a variety of changes ranging from the rate – later charge – capping of some authorities to the abolition of others. The responsibilities of local authorities in the area of education were reduced by the direct funding of schools. Nevertheless, local authorities still take many significant decisions and therefore become the focus of pressure-group activity. Occasionally, the actions of a local authority may attract the attention of a national pressure group such as the CBI. More generally, however, the pressure group is purely local in character. A considerable number of organisations exist at the local level: Newton (1976) identified 4,264 in his study of Birmingham. Many of these organisations are not primarily political in character. For example, they may be engaged in a variety of leisure activities ranging from swimming to ballroom dancing. However, such groups may become actively involved in local politics if their activities are threatened in some way – if, for example, an allotment society or a football club is told that its council-owned site is to be developed for housing.

In such cases, existing organisations with memberships and funds can be mobilised to lobby councillors, and officers become drawn into the local political process. In many other cases, a loose campaigning group is formed to fight on a particular issue such as a projected school closure, a new road, or a new development. Once the issue is resolved one way or the other, the group dissolves. Relatively informal groupings of this kind are emerging and disappearing all the time at the local level; in one sense, they could be regarded as a healthy flowering of local democracy, although they often lack the resources and inside knowledge available to the decision-makers. Moreover, such groups are often seeking to protect rather narrow interests, so that 'sporadic interventionism' assumes a 'highly individual and unorganised form with affected people arguing against one another for personal compensation and benefit' (Dowse and Hughes 1977, p. 90).

Many local campaigning organisations are closely linked with political parties, especially the Labour Party. Seyd and Whiteley's survey of Labour Party members (1992) shows that 18.8 per cent of those surveyed were also members of a local community action group, and 16.5 per cent were members of a local tenants' or housing group (p. 92). Indignant citizens may also form their own local single-issue party, not in a serious effort to win seats, but to demonstrate strength of support for their cause. For example, supporters of Charlton Athletic football club formed 'the Valley Party' as part of an effort to overcome opposition from Greenwich

Council to the return of the club to its historic home at the Valley ground.

There are, however, some more permanent primary pressure groups at the local level. One important category is the local amenity society, which may be a branch of the CPRE or may have a purely local title such as 'The Henley Society' or 'The Leamington Society'. By 1975 there were about 1,200 such societies throughout the country (Lowe and Goyder 1983, p. 89). For a variety of reasons, including the technical knowledge possessed by their members, their 'responsible' stance, and their appeal to broadly based values rather than narrow interests, such organisations tend to have a close working relationship with their local authorities. 'Some environmental groups such as the Ancient Monuments Society, the Georgian Society and the Victorian Society have developed insider status to the point where they have to be consulted as a matter of statute by the local planning authorities before a listed building is altered or demolished.' (Robinson 1992, p. 38)

Another important category of local pressure group is the chamber of commerce or chamber of trade, representing local business interests. Chambers of trade have traditionally been organisations of local retailers, with perhaps some membership from other small business interests, while chambers of commerce have a much broader membership including large businesses in the locality. The larger chambers of commerce have considerable resources and substantial staffs (for example, well over a hundred in Birmingham). In smaller urban centres, however, chambers may not have any paid staff.

However, it is clear that some of the more effective chambers have developed a close, insider-group relationship with their local authorities. For example, a study of the Norwich chamber found that all major planning applications were shown to the chamber, and city and chamber officials made a joint site visit where commercial sites were involved (Grant 1983). Chambers have also become closely involved in the implementation of inner-city policy, as 'local authorities are obliged by the [Department of the Environment] to consult Chambers of Commerce before schemes to be included in the urban programme can go forward to central government' (King 1985, p. 207). Under the Conservative governments of the 1980s and 1990s chambers of commerce tended to acquire new responsibilities in relation to local authorities, being seen as the authentic voice of the small entrepreneur and as a means of restraining any excesses by local government. They may house local 'one-stop shop' offices set up by the DTI.

In rural areas, farmers and landowners are an important interest, often, of course, directly represented in significant numbers on local authorities. A study of Suffolk found that there was a close, harmonious and informal relationship between the National Farmers' Union and the Country Landowners' Association on the one hand, and the planning authorities on the other. The following was observed:

> the agricultural interest and the 'public interest' are synonymous, or are at least seen to be so. Indeed, the identification drawn by local and county planners between the two has resulted in a marked reluctance on the part of local authorities to invoke such powers as they may have in order to force farmers to observe regulations which may hinder the profitability of agricultural enterprises.
>
> (Newby et al. 1978, p. 235)

However, in the 1980s and 1990s, the influx of middle-class incomers from an urban background has changed the character of many rural localities. Such individuals are often prepared to complain about planning infringements, or breaches of environmental regulations, by farmers to local authorities. The latest round of local government reorganisation may also further reduce the influence of the rural interest in some areas.

Environmental groups have considerably increased their activities at the local level. This can be seen in part as a response to the trend for local authorities to be 'some of the most active institutions in responding to the upsurge in interest in environmental problems' (Ward 1993, p. 453). This does, of course, provide local authorities with a new and potentially popular – but not too costly – sphere of activity which can serve to offset all the areas where their responsibilities have been eroded. Friends of the Earth, above all other pressure groups, 'has been crucially important in both stimulating and feeding off local authority interest' (p. 471). Ward argues that Friends of the Earth has adopted a more constructive style, offering solutions and practical advice as well as criticism. This 'change in attitude of FoE stems partly from frustration with national government and the lack of ability to gain influence in Whitehall' (p. 473). There has been a shift from an outsider towards an insider relationship:

> Both sides are still wary of one another and tensions do remain; local authorities are still cautious about the possible unpredictable nature of FoE . . . . Equally FoE activists are uneasy about becoming too deeply involved in governing structures . . . . However, FoE has undoubtedly gained a certain degree of respect from local government and is increasingly involved at the centre of local government forums.
>
> (Ward 1993, p. 472)

Some areas have trade councils which bring together trade unions in the locality, but they have tended to diminish in significance over time. In practice, the public-sector unions such as Unison are an important force in defending the interests of their members, which can include opposing major changes in local-authority policy that involve cutbacks in services.

The voluntary sector (for example Councils for Voluntary Service, Age Concern) is of increasing importance at the local level, particularly as it is often responsible for the delivery of services funded by the local authority. Stoker (1991, pp. 124–8) argues that 'given the rise of self-help organisations within the sector and a more general willingness to engage in campaigning activity, the potential for and likely effectiveness of voluntary sector lobbying of local authorities has also been considerably enhanced'. The transformation of local government in the direction of an 'enabling' model (Brooke 1989), which leads to more emphasis on partnerships with the private and voluntary sectors, creates a new class of 'insider' groups whose involvement in service delivery gives them a special opportunity to influence policy development.

In many ways, the distinction between insider and outsider groups has often seemed to be more marked at the local than at the national level. Policy is largely formed through discussions between officers and councillors, but some groups may be granted an established consultative relationship, if only as a means of explaining the local authority's policy to interested audiences. Moreover, there has been a more general opening-out by at least some authorities, which provides new opportunities for interest-group activity and influence (see Stoker 1988, pp. 120–4). What is clear is that there is considerable variation from one local authority area to another, in terms of both the patterns of interest-group activity and the receptiveness of local councils to their representations.

While emphasising the uneven development, diversity and complexity of relationships between pressure groups and local authorities, Stoker (1991) sets up a helpful fivefold typology:

1. Left-wing Labour authorities in urban areas. A strong emphasis on good relations with trade unions and tenants', ethnic minority and other community groups, but there are often antagonistic relations with business groups.
2. 'Soft left' councils which 'are less likely to support radical cause groups and more willing to work with business interests' (p. 133).
3. Urban areas with centre-right Labour or Liberal Democrat influenced authorities. These authorities seek to work with a wide range of groups, but may be suspicious of some, such as tenants' associations thought to have extremist links, or residents' associations thought to be concerned with a narrow, middle-class agenda.
4. Suburban or rural locations where Conservative and Liberal Democrat councils predominate. Farming interests will be well established, and there will be a growing voice for the environmental and amenity lobby, but some cause groups may be viewed as unacceptable, such as those campaigning for the homeless.
5. 'New Right' Conservative authorities which are willing to work with business interests, residents' associations and amenity societies, but are hostile to campaigning organisations perceived to be left-wing, including 'elements of the voluntary sector that are viewed as "political"' (p. 134).

Stoker's approach, which emphasises the politics of the controlling party as the key variable, provides an alternative to conceptualisations of local-authority decision-making in terms of a technocratic model that emphasises the power that officers derive from their professional expertise, or the sharing of power by a joint élite of senior councillors and officers (see Wilson 1988). Whichever model one adopts, however, the extent to which pressure groups are able to exert influence is significantly affected by the attitudes towards them of councillors and/or local-authority officers.

In general, there is not the same tradition of long-term, routine consultation as at the national level. This is accentuated by the fact that local pressure groups generally have fewer resources in terms of their own staff than their national counterparts, whilst local-authority officers are less dependent on them as a source of information and consent than civil servants. Although citizen groups fighting local-authority policies often have an uphill battle, there is scope for pressure-group activity at the local level. As a number of the examples discussed suggest, the range and sophistication of such activity would appear to be growing.

6

Pressure groups and the European Union

Pressure groups concentrate their activities where the power is. As the Single European Act and the Maastricht treaty have broadened the competences of the European Union, and reduced the range of questions that have to be resolved by unanimity through the extended use of qualified majority voting, pressure groups have increasingly switched their attention to Brussels. One estimate suggests that the number of people employed by pressure groups in Brussels doubled from 5,000 at the end of the 1980s to 10,000 in 1994 (*Financial Times*, 9 April 1994). Given that the European Commission (EC) has around 10,000 officials, excluding translators and central administrative services, this gives a ratio of roughly one pressure-group employee to every Commission official. Business groups have been by far the more successful operators at the European level, in spite of subsidies paid by the European Union to non-governmental organisations operating in other areas. In particular, large multinational companies have opened their own offices in Brussels, and have had a substantial influence on the formation of more effective European-level business organisations.

The agricultural lobby has been a classic focus of the study of pressure groups at the EU level because it has always had a special place in the decision-making process at the European level. Even in the mid-1990s, the Common Agricultural Policy (CAP) accounts for over half the budget. However, agricultural organisations such as

COPA (Committee of Professional Agricultural Associations) have found it increasingly difficult to maintain unity around effective policies as tensions between Northern and Southern European countries and between different commodities have been intensified by budget cuts and reforms. These problems would be compounded by EU enlargement: indeed, it is doubtful whether the CAP could survive a substantial enlargement of the Union which brought in countries outside what used to be thought of as Western Europe. A Commission source is quoted in one study as saying, 'Agriculture will have to start lobbying in a different way to protect its interests, as there is an enormous upheaval to come.' (Burson-Marsteller 1991, p. 16)

In the 1990s the focus of work has turned away from agriculture to the general expansion of pressure-group activity at the EU level, particularly in terms of business organisation, with important empirical work being undertaken by Mazey and Richardson (1992a–b, 1993a–d). Yet in many respects the overall research picture remains unsatisfactory:

> forty years of scientific research on the subject . . . does not add up to a coherent picture of the nature of interest organization in the EC. There is little consensus about the importance of different types of interest groups, about the influence they can exert on the politics and policies of the EC and the effect their activities have on the development of the integration process.
>
> (Kohler-Koch 1994, p. 166)

Kohler-Koch notes (1994, p. 166) 'that most research has concentrated on case-studies trying to evaluate the influence of pressure groups on decision-making in a particular policy-field'. Particularly if the case studies are not firmly located in an analytical framework, it is easy to slip into the fallacy of basing a generalisation on what may be an untypical particular example. Although there has been a concern with whether groups have been able to play the positive role in the process of unification assigned to them by integration theorists, and debates about the relative merits of pluralist and corporatist models, the debate has generally been atheoretical. It is, of course, difficult to theorise about a political process that is in a state of constant evolution, of which the final outcome is uncertain, and which in the meantime is often characterised by unpredictability. Nevertheless, the point may have arrived for some new efforts at theory-building. One unorthodox departure point might be to work on understanding the firm as an actor which needs to be analysed in terms of its political strategies and perceptions of the future development of Europe, rather than just simply as a profit maximiser or a set of organisational relationships, important though these aspects are.

Some caution is necessary in approaching the existing literature on pressure groups at the European Union level. One of the defects of much of the existing literature on European integration is that it has been written by authors who tend to take a relatively benign and uncritical view of the integration process. An emergent conventional wisdom in debates about public policy has been that the nation-state is likely to be supplanted by transnational structures on the one hand, and sub-regional arrangements on the other. This view is premature at the least. There is also a specific danger inherent in the study of European-level pressure groups. In focusing on them as an object of study, it is very easy to emphasise their achievements, and to place less emphasis on their limits.

In this chapter, the various strategies and forms of organisation available to interests seeking to influence decision-making at the EU level will be reviewed. The relative importance of the various targets of pressure-group activity at the EU level – the Commission, the Parliament, the Court of Justice – will be assessed. The analysis will then turn to the strengths of business interests at the European level, and the relative weakness of environmental and other interests. The chapter will conclude with a review of prospects for future development, together with an assessment of experiments in corporatist forms of decision-making at the EU level.

The decline of the national route?

One means of exerting influence at the EU level has always been for a national pressure group to persuade its government to adopt its policy position on a particular issue and to press for it in the Council of Ministers. It is worth remembering that the European Union's decision-making procedures 'are still prescribed by the final say of the member states in the Council. Intergovernmental negotiations and compromises, be it under unanimity or qualified majority voting rules, are at the core of Community politics.' (Arp 1993, p. 163)

Any group that relied solely on its tried-and-tested links with the national government has always been taking a substantial risk. First, the national government has to be convinced of the desirability of adopting the lobby's position. Persuading 'the UK Government to identify with a particular interest is potentially dependent on political considerations going beyond the specific issue concerned' (Spence 1993, p. 52). Second, 'Positions are watered down during the domestic co-ordination process and in negotiation with the Commission and other member states.' (p. 49) In the final stage of bargaining in long and exhausting negotiating sessions in the Council of Ministers, the group's position may be suddenly abandoned by the national government in order to resolve a problem elsewhere. Domestic sheep farmers may find themselves abandoned in the interests of New Zealand lamb imports, or vice versa. Third, if the matter is a relatively technical one, the national government representatives may not appreciate its full significance. For example, 'a British minister disappointed national groups when he inadvertently agreed to unacceptable technical proposals during bargaining over emissions regulations' (McLaughlin, Jordan and Maloney 1993, pp. 197–8).

Greenwood, Grote and Ronit (1992, pp. 23–4) have argued that 'The importance of the national route appears in fact to have been somewhat overstated . . . there is an increasing confidence and familiarity with the European level, and . . . the "Brussels strategy" . . . is increasingly being taken.' Similarly, Mazey and Richardson argue that an exclusive reliance on a national-level strategy is no longer a viable option. 'With qualified majority voting, a *European* lobbying strategy becomes essential for groups *in addition* to the maintenance and strengthening of links with national officials.' (Mazey and Richardson 1993a, p. 15)

Even after enlargement takes place, the threshold required to succeed under the qualified majority voting arrangements (which do not apply to all decisions) will still be relatively high. Even so, the existence of qualified majority voting provides an additional incentive to abandon rigid national positions and reach a bargained compromise. One does, however, have to balance the importance of institutional changes in the European Union against the extent to which the integration process is being driven by the interests and perceptions of large multinational companies. One government relations manager in a multinational company observed in interview that his company wanted 'to break down borders between member states because we want to move goods about'. If multinationals decide that the logic of production and marketing means they want an effective European political entity, they will adjust their political operations accordingly.

It is important to remember, however, that the European Union has very little in the way of implementation and enforcement capability. It is dependent on the member states to implement directives. For example, by April 1994, over a year after the start of the internal market, every member state had failed to implement all the relevant directives, with the number outstanding ranging from eleven in Denmark to forty-four in Greece, with twenty-three measures not notified in the case of Britain *(The Economist*, 21 May 1994). As far as enforcement is concerned, environmental groups seek to act as 'whistle-blowers' by 'warning the Commission of implementation failure at the national level' (Mazey and Richardson 1992b, p. 126). Because translating Union directives into action on the ground is the task of the member states, a range of possibilities is opened up for exemption, delay and modification which can be highly beneficial to particular interests. As Sargent notes (1993, p. 235) damage limitation is the speciality of trade associations:

> Damage-limitation activities may involve attempts to limit the scope of a particular piece of legislation, to exempt a category of companies altogether, or to remove from the scope of a proposal some of a company's most sensitive products . . . . At other times, attention focuses on taking action to achieve as late an implementation date as possible, in order to avoid the consequences of being unable to meet the requirements of the original deadline.

The bathing water directive is a classic example of the way in which a national government may frustrate the intentions of a directive by interpreting it in a way which nullifies its purpose. After the directive was ratified in 1976, the British government issued guidelines for the identification of bathing waters which required more than 1,500 people in the water per mile for a beach to be defined as bathing water. As a result only twenty-seven bathing waters were identified in the whole country, less than in

Luxembourg which has no coast. Following pressure from the Commission, the number of bathing waters was increased to nearly 400 by 1987. However, complaints about the UK's practical compliance with the directive in places like Blackpool led to the Commission bringing the matter before the European Court. The Court clarified what was meant by bathing water in terms of facilities such as toilets and changing-huts. The initial discretion given to Britain and other member states has been considerably restricted by the Court's judgement in 1993, but this was seventeen years after the original directive. More generally, this example shows the reactive nature of enforcement powers, the limited resources of the Commission, and the dependence of the monitoring process on information provided by the member states (Somsen 1994). There are many ways in which the application of a directive can be delayed and diverted over many years.

Effective European lobbying has always depended on using the full range of methods available in whatever mix appears appropriate to the particular case. Strategy and tactics may change as the particular issue evolves. An interest which is not represented at the European level is not going to be able to cope with the unpredictability of the decision-making process in Brussels, where a draft directive may suddenly be taken from the piles of paper on an official's desk and launched on a new stage of its life. As was noted in an earlier chapter, a pensioners' organisation was unable to influence the British government effectively from Blackburn. Communications between London and Brussels are better, but there is no substitute for an effective presence in Brussels.

Even so, it is important to remember how deeply Brussels politics is still coloured by the pursuit of national interest. This is evident in the manoeuvring that accompanies the allocation of Commission portfolios, or in the selection of a new Commission president. It is not confined, however, to major decisions at the highest level. The author represents Britain on a minor EU management committee where national interests frequently surface when decisions have to be made. On those more important bodies which have professional rather than amateur members, 'where a lobby can persuade government of its cause, the efficiency and the strength of the machinery of UK European policy-making makes UK officialdom a very strong ally' (Spence 1993, p. 71).

National groups still recognise that 'they must be careful not to alienate their own ministries by pursuing a contrary line to Brussels' (Mazey and Richardson 1993b, p. 247). National associations arrive at their European-level meetings with their national baggage in tow. It is only where European-wide multinationals are directly represented that these national perspectives can be cast aside.

The national route is most important in the evolving European Union once a directive has been issued and has to be implemented and enforced. Implementation studies in political science over the last twenty years have revealed the gap between legislation and what actually happens on the ground. These problems are compounded when one has a political system that is a confederation of nation-states with different interests and administrative systems that vary in their capacities and forms of organisation. Indeed, it is sometimes complained that Britain is too effective in implementing EU decisions.

Even in a long-established federal system like that of the United States, pressure groups use state governments to put pressure on the federal authorities (Grant, forthcoming). At the policy-formation stage, the national route is likely to remain one of a number of important routes used by pressure groups in the EU, while its use at the implementation stage may ease the pain of decisions that threaten particular interests. The position in the mid-1990s is well summarised by Greenwood and Jordan (1993) who argue that in a changing kaleidoscope the national level is the most important overall for political action aimed at the EC, but that the significance of European-level channels must not be underestimated, particularly in relation to policy formulation.

European-level pressure groups

As the European Union has extended the range and depth of its responsibilities, an increasing number of associations of associations have been formed at the European level to represent particular interests. No one knows exactly how many there are, but in the chemicals sector alone (excluding pharmaceuticals), there are nine major sector and subsector associations and over 100 product groups (see Table 6.1). The European Council of Chemical Manufacturers' Federations (CEFIC) formed seven new product groups

Table 6.1   Examples of European-level federations representing the chemical industry (excluding pharmaceuticals)

Sector and subsector associations:

CEFIC (Conseil Européen des Fédérations de l'Industrie Chimique)
Association of Plastics Manufacturers in Europe (APME)
Association Internationale de la Savonnerie et de la Détergence (AIS)
Groupement International des Associations Nationales de Fabricants de
  Produits Agrochimiques (GIFAP) (global organisation)

Product-level associations:

Association of European Producers of Sporting Ammunition (AFEMS)
Cadmium Pigment Producers Association (CPA)
European Council of Vinyl Manufacturers (ECVM)
European Methylbromide Association (EMA)
Zinc Oxide Producers Association (ZOPA)

---

in 1991 alone. For example, the European Producers of Anti-microbial Substances was formed by fifteen companies concerned with non-agricultural pesticides to defend their interests in relation to a proposed directive on the subject.

Mazey and Richardson (1993a, p. 6) report that there are now 525 Euro-groups recognised by the Commission, while Grote puts the figure at over 700 (quoted in Greenwood and Jordan 1993, p. 82). It is difficult to arrive at a reliable figure, as many smaller organisations are in effect 'letterhead' operations which share staff and premises with kindred organisations and spring into being when a particular interest is endangered, and the appropriate headed notepaper is inserted into the printer.

Most of these European-level groups are relatively ineffective. Writing from the perspective of a Commission official, Hull (1993) comments (p. 82), 'Where good lobbying takes place, it is the exception and it tends to stand out very clearly.' Drawing on their extensive research, Mazey and Richardson argue (1993a, p. 15) 'despite the proliferation of Euro-lobbying there are still relatively few really *effective* EC lobbyists'. Despite the preference of the European Commission for dealing with Europe-wide groups that can represent a sector or interest across the whole Union, Euro-groups 'have tended to be rather ineffective bodies unable to engage in constructive policy dialogue with the Commission' (McLaughlin, Jordan and Maloney 1993, p. 192).

Why should this be the case? First, the problem of reconciling the interests of the different member states under what are often unanimity rules of decision-making means that the groups tend to produce 'lowest common denominator' policies which are unlikely to have an effective impact on decision-makers. Second, given that they are funded by national associations who want to retain a large proportion of their income for their own purposes, the associations often have insufficient resources to deal with the large range of issues that impact on their sectors. Third, whereas an effective association will be guided by the knowledge of its officials about what is and is not achievable in the decision-making process, too many of the organisations are membership led: the logic of membership predominates over the logic of influence. European-level officials have insufficient autonomy in relation to either national-level associations or multinational companies who may regard them as middle-ranking bureaucrats.

Nevertheless, there are examples of federations of federations which 'can act coherently and decisively' (Greenwood, Grote and Ronit 1992, p. 6). How is it that some Euro-level federations are able to rise above their difficulties and operate as effective organisations? An examination of CEFIC – which is viewed as one of the most effective sectoral-level groups – may help to provide some of the answers.

The chemical industry has a number of characteristics which predispose it to effective common organisation. It is integrated in terms of its forms of production, with many plants in Northern Europe being linked with each other by a network of pipelines. The production of industrial chemicals is undertaken by a relatively small number of companies which have been participants in the industry for a long time. It is therefore a relatively stable industry, and one in which there are fewer conflicts between large and small firms than in other sectors. In a capital-intensive industry, the leading firms have been able to find the resources to provide CEFIC with one of the largest staffs of any sector federation.

Many of the EU's activities have a considerable impact on the industry. It is particularly affected by the development of the Union's environmental policies, while competition policy is also very important for the industry. The rise of competing petrochemical industries in other parts of the world, such as the Far East, means that the EU's stance in General Agreement on Tariffs and

Trade (GATT) negotiations is a major concern for the industry, while the way in which the EU implements anti-dumping regulations to deal with surges of cheap imports is another central issue.

The emergence of CEFIC as an effective federation, however, has not just happened as an automatic response to the characteristics of the industry and the problems it faces. It has involved deliberate choices about organisational design made by key leaders from the multinational companies involved in CEFIC, working with CEFIC staff. In particular, CEFIC has taken steps to involve the large multinational firms directly in the work of the organisation. The first steps in this direction were taken under the presidency of Sir John Harvey-Jones of ICI in 1985. In 1991 CEFIC gave full membership to companies and developed a bicameral structure which created a shared balance of power between its historic national federation members and the individual chemical companies. These steps were not easy, as they met with some resistance from the German chemical association, the *Verband der Chemischen Industrie*. Germany has a strong tradition of action through associations rather than by individual companies, while the latter has been more usual in Britain. The German association was also concerned to protect the interests of its small and medium-sized company members and to prevent the emergence of conflicts between large and small firms at national and European levels (Kohler-Koch 1993, p. 37).

Direct membership associations

As multinational companies have become increasingly dissatisfied with the performance of federations of associations, they have formed direct membership associations of companies in some sectors. These are a particularly significant development, representing a more mature form of interest representation at the EU level. They are more likely to be able to formulate meaningful policies based on a Europe-wide perspective.

In 1991 the European motor industry formed a new unified organisation to represent the sector, the Association of European Automobile Constructors (ACEA). 'Within ACEA, voting power resides with the fifteen member companies in the Board of Directors and there has been a marginalization of the role of trade associations.' (McLaughlin and Jordan 1993, p. 147) One of the significant features of the new organisation was that it abandoned the unanimity rule and adopted majority voting with a 75 per cent threshold. One of the industry participants interviewed by McLaughlin, Jordan and Maloney commented, ' "We have succeeded in moving away from the lowest common denominator towards a policy package which accommodated the various industry positions." ' (McLaughlin, Jordan and Maloney 1993, p. 206)

The new organisation includes the American and Swedish manufacturers, but not the Japanese, and was largely formed in response to the need to establish a common position on the question of Japanese imports. It would seem that the final impetus towards the formation of a new organisation came from the Commission, confirming the observation that it is frequently the state or its equivalent that is able to bring about group reorganisation. 'By early 1991, the Commission insisted that the industry speak with one voice before the key negotiations started with the Japanese government.' (McLaughlin, Jordan and Maloney 1993, p. 206)

PSA (Peugeot Citroën) decided to remain outside the group because it favoured a tougher line against the Japanese. It is, however, difficult for a major company to remain outside a group of this kind – and lose its opportunity to influence the development of policy – and so PSA joined in March 1994. Peugeot was apparently concerned that it might become isolated from future pan-European research and development projects in the motor industry *(Financial Times*, 27 March 1994).

As part of the Harvey-Jones reforms in the chemical sector, a separate organisation to represent the large petrochemicals producers was set up within CEFIC. Membership is confined to multinational companies, who have to be represented at meetings by senior executives. In its early years, the Association of Petrochemicals Producers in Europe (APPE) focused on the overcapacity problem which was besetting the European industry. Although it could not become directly involved in resolving the problem, it was able to provide the context within which companies could tackle the problem through capacity swaps, joint ventures and other measures. Its role in the early 1990s is perhaps less clearly defined.

CEFIC was also involved in the formation of another direct membership association made up of a small number of multinational companies, the Senior Advisory Group Biotechnology (SAGB). It has proved to be an 'intense and effective lobbyist in Brussels' (Greenwood and Ronit 1992, p. 91) and these authors conclude (p. 94) that 'The SAGB provides an extremely important and influential example of large firm cooperation at the European level.' The membership was subsequently broadened beyond the seven founding members to encompass a number of smaller firms. SAGB has emphasised the development of high-level contacts in the Commission and other Union institutions. It has established a priority work programme and supported the development of a coherent European Union policy for biotechnology.

In some cases what may appear to be a federation of federations may function more like a direct membership association. In the consumer electronics industry, Philips is a member of all nine national trade associations represented in the European Association of Consumer Electronics Manufacturers (EACEM) and Thomson is a member of five (Cawson 1992, p. 108). EACEM acquired a permanent secretariat in 1990. 'The advantage for Philips and Thomson of a strengthened EACEM lies in the public cloak of legitimacy through which their interests can be credibly argued to be representative of the industry as a whole.' (Cawson 1992, p. 110)

Direct membership associations have so far formed in just a few industrial sectors, and they are organisations of firms not citizens. Are there any particular sectoral conditions which favour the formation of such associations? First, the industry should have a strong international orientation in terms of its structure and marketing strategies. The industry will be one in which 'global firms responding to changing international marketing conditions and engaged in a complex network of relationships with other firms are the crucial actors' (Martinelli and Grant 1991, p. 297). Second, the sector's activities should be substantially influenced by decisions taken by the EU: for example, the sector should be one for which the internal market is of key importance. Third, it should have a relatively small number of large firms, facilitating cooperation and ensuring that the resources for an effective association are available. These conditions are met in sectors such as chemicals, consumer electronics and motor vehicles. Examples of sectors in which they are not met include construction, furniture manufacture and hotels.

The targets of representation

The European Commission is the principal target of pressure groups operating at the European level. More precisely, the target is Commission services, with 3,500 or so senior administrators (10,000 counting middle-rank officials involved in policy work) who work in the twenty-three directorates-general dealing with particular aspects of the work of the European Union such as internal market and industrial affairs or environmental policy. Leading pressure groups such as the CBI have direct meetings with individual commissioners, but this level of access is not available to most groups. Rather more common is the practice of making contact with the cabinets, or teams of personal advisers, that assist each commissioner. Because coordination between different directorates-general is not as well developed as between government departments in Britain, many conflicts between different spheres of responsibility have to be settled at this level. The author's interviews in Brussels indicate that access to cabinets is available to leading companies and groups. 'This is a real opportunity, since a considerable amount of political horse-trading takes place between Commissioners. It is, however, a fairly unreliable way of influencing a proposal and can never guarantee results.' (Hull 1993, p. 84)

If the decision-making process in the Commission is highly political at the highest levels, it is generally relatively technical at the lower levels, giving pressure groups opportunities to press for their definition of the problem under consideration to be incorporated in the Commission working document which forms the basis of the decision-making process. The average Commission official has a wide range of matters to deal with, and insufficient time and expertise to cope with them adequately on his or her own. A Commission official commented:

> We are terribly understaffed and overstressed. My division is responsible for 44 directives and 89 regulations; monthly mail which requires a substantial answer numbers about 350 pieces. And I have about nine staff to deal with all of this. The corresponding administration in the [United] States has 600 people.
> (Quoted in Burston-Marsteller 1991, p. 22)

The combination of a high workload and often relatively young officials with little outside experience provides an opportunity for the pressure group that can offer information and expertise at an early stage of the process of policy formation:

> At the beginning he or she is a very lonely official with a blank piece of paper, wondering what to put on it. Lobbying at this very early stage offers the greatest opportunity to shape thinking and ultimately to shape policy. The drafter is usually in need of ideas and information and a lobbyist who is recognized as being trustworthy and a provider of good information can have an important impact at this stage. Thereafter, once the Commission itself has agreed a proposal and sent it to the Parliament and Council, scope for changing the proposal exists only at the margin, involving about 20 per cent of the total proposal.
>
> (Hull 1993, p. 83)

Most bureaucracies are internally divided, and the European Commission is probably less monolithic than most. Each directorate-general has its own bureaucratic mission, so the competition directorate (DG IV) may take a more legalistic, arm's-length approach than DG III (internal market and industrial affairs). DG V (social policy) is seen as more open to the unions, and DG XI (environment) is perceived as more likely to listen to environmentalists. However, one business association official commented in an interview, 'DG XI are reasonably receptive . . . . They're never averse to communication and information. They are inclined to be a little bit idealistic.'

Within a particular directorate-general, one individual may be more responsive to outside representations than another. Informal links may develop with Commission officials from the country of a pressure group, or between staff in a Euro-level group and their fellow nationals in the Commission. For Germans, 'A particular way of thinking along certain cultural lines – quite apart from language problems – explains the preference for communication with German Commission staff.' (Kohler-Koch 1993, p. 39) A Flemish government relations manager commented in interview, 'UK people are easier to lobby than anyone else. Maybe this is because the UK is more influenced by the US where lobbying is a qualified profession.'

There may be greater variations than in a national bureaucracy in terms of the approaches to their job of individual Commission officials. In interviews with lobbyists in Brussels, particular individuals in the Commission have often been referred to as easier to deal with than others. The European Union 'has not yet created a unified bureaucratic ideology or operational style . . . the Commission does not at present practise anything like the "standard operating procedures" which are usual in Britain and Scandinavia . . . for the managing of the interface between groups and government' (Mazey and Richardson 1993c, p. 117).

Before policy proposals are considered by the relevant Council of Ministers, they will be inspected by the Committee of Permanent Representatives (COREPER) made up of each member state's representative in Brussels. Proposals are first examined by a working party of experts from the relevant government departments of the member states, along with a Commission representative. 'In this stage of decision-making the national administration is again the main target of interest representation.' (Kohler-Koch 1993, p. 39) Through the work of these bodies, the areas of disagreement between member states can be narrowed, and issues sifted into those which are relatively non-contentious and those which will have to be the subject of ministerial discussion. If the working party can agree, the proposal goes to COREPER for its assent, and is passed to the Council under the 'A'–list procedure. If the working group cannot agree, and COREPER cannot resolve the problem, it goes to the Council for discussion as a 'B'–list item. Another key coordinating body is the Antici group which brings together one official from each member state's permanent representation, the head of the Commission division dealing with the Council and a delegate from the Council Secretariat.

Members of COREPER do not, however, wait until items appear on the agenda in front of them before deciding how to deal with them. The officials in the UK permanent representation 'maintain close contacts with their opposite numbers in the Commission, forming a kind of permanent UK lobby with the aim of influencing the Commission's forward thinking and obtaining early warning of proposals and modifications to the Commission's negotiating position' (Spence 1993, pp. 66–7). The permanent representation 'is thus a prime focus for the private-sector lobby' (p. 66). As well as being another route through which developments in Commission thinking may be influenced at an early stage, 'there is evidence of private exchanges with national permanent delegations at COREPER resulting in influence being exerted through the European Council' (Greenwood, Grote and Ronit 1992, p. 19).

The Council of Ministers is 'ultimately the most powerful EC institution, yet it remains relatively insulated from the *direct* influence of groups' (Mazey and Richardson 1993a, p. 17). Of course, particularly in the case of the Council of Agricultural Ministers, the ministers themselves may be embedded in a policy community which ties them closely to particular client groups. In the case of agriculture, however, the imperatives of the EU's budgetary problems, and the need to reach a successful conclusion in the international trade negotiations known as the Uruguay Round, meant that agricultural ministers pressed ahead with significant reforms to the CAP. When ministers enter the council chamber, intergovernmental bargaining becomes paramount, and there is a sense in which even the most influential interest groups become outsiders.

The Maastricht treaty has substantially enhanced the powers of the European Parliament, yet for most groups it has remained a secondary rather than a primary focus of lobbying activity. It has been particularly used by groups which might have difficulty in pressing their case elsewhere in the Union's institutions and which have some public support which can be mobilised to exert pressure on Members of the European Parliament (MEPs). For example, some of the successes of the animal welfare lobby have been achieved 'through the Parliament more than the other institutions' (Harvey 1993, p. 197).

Business groups have often subcontracted European Parliament representation to a lobbying firm, although CEFIC appointed a full-time liaison officer in 1990. This decision reflects an increasing realisation that business interests will have to pay more systematic attention to the Parliament, particularly to its committees. Higher-calibre individuals are being elected, although the benefits of this are to some extent offset by higher turnover than in the Commission. The new Parliament elected in 1994 is likely to want to try and exercise the additional powers given to it by the Maastricht treaty.

The number of lobbyists working in Brussels and Strasbourg to build relations with MEPs was estimated in 1994 to be 140 public-affairs consultancies, 160 law firms, 572 trade and professional associations and 58 regional and local authorities (*Financial Times*, 26 May 1994). Increasing concern about the number of lobbyists in the Parliament, and the methods of some of them, has led to the introduction of a measure to require them to register and operate under a formal code of conduct.

The European Court of Justice offers another route for groups which lack insider status:

> In recent years, environmental organisations, trade unions and women's groups especially have used the Court as a means of forcing recalcitrant national governments to implement EC legislation on matters such as state aids, the quality of drinking water and equal pay and treatment of male and female employees.
>
> (Mazey and Richardson 1993a, p. 19)

While the Court may be useful in establishing particular decisions which may have far-reaching implications, 'access to the European Court is very restricted. Moreover, it is difficult to control the implementation of the decisions of the Court.' (Rucht 1993, p. 88)

The Economic and Social Committee was the body specifically set up to represent interests under the Treaty of Rome, but it is of marginal importance. Even when the European Union has moved in the direction of more corporatist arrangements, it has preferred to work through less cumbersome bodies such as the Tripartite Conferences of the 1970s. Streeck and Schmitter (1991, p. 138) note: 'there is general agreement that it has, in fact, accomplished very little. In particular, it was never able to serve as a privileged access point for organized interests to European-level decision making.' It is the Commission that remains the key access point for pressure groups 'because the Commission is the only EC institution which is involved in each of the different stages of the policy cycle, from agenda-setting to the formulation and implementation of a policy' (Kohler-Koch 1993, p. 39).

The leading role of big business

Big-business interests dominate the pressure-group scene in Brussels. There are more of them, they are better resourced, and they have better contacts. Of the 518 groups analysed by Kohler-Koch (1994, p. 170), 416 may be placed in the business category (representing industry, commerce and the services). The next biggest group is the professions (fifty-nine), followed by eighteen trade-union organisations, ten representing small and medium-sized enterprises or the craft sector, eight concerned with transport and seven consumer groups.

There has already been a discussion of sectoral business associations, but the general business associations that seek to represent business as a whole are particularly important in any assessment of its influence on strategic issues. Representing business within a particular country is difficult enough, given the conflicts of interest between different sectors and large and small firms. These difficulties are multiplied at the European level.

It is therefore not surprising that the Union of Industrial and Employers' Confederations of Europe (UNICE) has encountered difficulties in establishing itself as an effective 'peak association' for European employers' associations. One government relations manager commented in interview, 'UNICE was felt to be useless, a federation of federations, a lowest common denominator.' In the early 1980s, a group of government affairs managers from leading multinationals, headed by Paul Winby, the Brussels government relations manager of ICI, set out to seek reforms in UNICE. With Lord Pennock of ICI as chairman, and Ziegmund Tyskiewicz brought in from Shell as secretary-general, UNICE began to streamline its decision-making structures and increase its influence. In 1990 UNICE set up an Advisory and Support Group (USAG) made up of multinational companies. Although partly a device to raise money, this grouping was also seen as a way of building closer links between UNICE and major companies. UNICE is a much more effective organisation than it used to be, but its problems are far from being solved:

> The great breadth of business interests clustered under UNICE's capacious umbrella . . . results in a somewhat bureaucratized decisionmaking process and an unfortunate softening of focus in the EC legislative area. Eurocrats frequently complain about bland consensus statements from UNICE which fail to address the specifics of proposed legislation.
>
> (Gardner 1991, p. 40)

To some extent, UNICE's revival has been stimulated by competition from the EC Committee of the American Chamber of Commerce, a direct membership body which represents the interests of American companies operating in Europe. Set up in its present form in 1985, the Committee has a young and energetic secretariat who have a reputation for responding quickly to issues and for carefully cultivating contacts with EU institutions.

In some ways, Brussels is more like Washington than London as a locale for lobbying. It is characterised by openness, informality, the relative accessibility of decision-makers, and a complexity and fluidity in decision-making structures. According to Mazey and Richardson (1992b, p. 112), 'the process is best described as policy-making through loose, open, and extended issue networks, rather than through well defined, stable and exclusive policy communities'. American companies may have a greater awareness of what lobbying requires than many of their European counterparts. It is worth noting that two of the most effective sectoral associations, ACEA and CEFIC, have admitted the Americans as members. The awareness of the staff of the American companies of the particular features of the American and European political settings may give the EC Committee a special set of advantages:

> As subsidiaries of *American* companies they are familiar with the practice of legislative advocacy in its Washington DC form. As *European* subsidiaries, managed and staffed primarily by Europeans, they have been able to adapt traditional lobbying techniques to the very different culture of legislative advocacy in Europe. The EC Committee has been remarkably successful in creating a hybrid form of lobbying – clear, unambiguous, fact-based presentations – with the low key, accommodating style favored by Europeans.
>
> (Gardner 1991, p. 43)

In many ways, the most effective business organisation has been the European Round Table (ERT) set up in 1983. It brings together around forty-five chief executives of leading European companies. Membership is by invitation only, with the membership list reading like a 'Who's Who of European industry' (Danton de Rouffignac 1991, p. 146). Plenary sessions are held twice a year, with a steering committee of five and a secretariat in Brussels. The Round Table has enjoyed direct access to the Commission president and other commissioners, as well as heads of government.

The formation of such a grouping was encouraged by the then industry commissioner, Viscount Davignon, and 'the first list of potential industry members was drawn up in the Berlaymont building' (Green 1993, p. 9). It was hoped that it would give a new momentum to the process of European integration. There has been some controversy about the extent to which the ERT was responsible for the

launch of the single market programme and the Single European
Act (Moravcsik 1991; Sandholtz and Zysman 1989). A carefully
researched and argued analysis concludes the following:

> the agenda for the Single Market program was largely set by the
> ERT . . . . Through their articulation of the need for European in-
> dustrial growth and the creation of European-scale projects, ERT
> members made it clear in direct meetings with government leaders
> why a unified market was vital . . . . When French government and
> Commission initiatives failed to produce a concrete proposal for a
> unified market, Wisse Dekker [the then ERT chairman from
> Philips] provided a solid plan. The ERT also proved to be an indis-
> pensable ally for Delors, Cockfield and the Commission when they
> undertook their policy initiatives in 1985.
>
> (Green 1993, p. 46)

The ERT has continued to be influential, not just because of the
economic and political standing of its élite members, but because it
has concentrated on a small number of important strategic issues
such as transport infrastructure and taxation, rather than attempting to cover every policy area. In December 1993, the ERT argued
that competitiveness should be placed at the top of the EU's political agenda. The ERT called for the creation of a US-style Competitiveness Council and a European Charter for Industry to serve as
a counterweight to social policy. Jacques Delors, the European
Commission president, attended the report's launch (*Financial
Times*, 4 December 1993).

The sophistication of business representation in Brussels has
been further enhanced by the widespread establishment of government relations offices by large companies. At least twenty-five
British companies had offices in Brussels in the mid-1990s, with an
informal grouping organised by the Brussels office of the CBI.
These offices act as listening posts for the companies to monitor
developments in Brussels which may affect their businesses. Their
staff can influence the activities of Euro-level associations but,
above all, they can engage in direct lobbying.

Another major development since the mid-1980s 'has been the
explosion in the number of professional lobbyists, financial consultants and law firms operating in Brussels' (Mazey and Richardson
1992a, p. 95). There are, for example, at least twenty American law
firms with Brussels offices. Companies active in the European
public-affairs field generally have a turnover of between £200,000

and £700,000, with the leading company claiming a turnover of £1 million (*Financial Times*, 26 May 1994). Lobbying intermediaries are often not well regarded in the Commission, as they would prefer to deal direct with the interest concerned, and there is some suspicion of their methods of operation. In an effort to make the lobbyists more professional, the European Institute of Public Affairs and Lobbying is offering a thirteen-week practical training course (*Financial Times*, 9 April 1994).

The dominance of business in the lobbying process in Brussels does give some cause for concern. Even if one believes in a free-enterprise market economy, there are other values and interests apart from those of business which need to be considered in the formation of public policy. The leading role of business interests in a business setting is not, of course, surprising. 'The most substantial problem with the pluralist approach is the tendency to treat business as just another group. Clearly, business has advantages that do not exist for other groups.' (Smith 1993, p. 27)

Alternative perspectives to those of business

The countervailing groups which represent different interests or outlooks to those of big business are all politically weaker. Although it was classified by the 1972 Paris Summit as one of the 'social partner' organisations, the trade union movement, represented by the European Trade Union Confederation (ETUC), has been relatively weak at the European level. Streeck and Schmitter argue (1991, p. 139) that 'there is no doubt that as a European actor labor is afflicted by *specific disabilities* that are not usually present at the national level and that do not in the same way affect business'. The member organisations, which have been to some extent divided on ideological lines, have generally been domestically oriented with a strong desire to preserve their own autonomy. 'While for unions from advanced countries a joint European strategy is unlikely to offer improvements over what they have already gained on their own, to unions from weaker countries common demands tend to appear unrealistically ambitious and remote from their everyday practical concerns.' (Streeck and Schmitter 1991, p. 140)

Perhaps because of a recognition of the importance of greater unity if EU policies are to be influenced, there has been an effort to build a policy consensus in recent years. A working group established in 1989 advocated substantial internal reforms within the ETUC, and in 1991 a two-thirds majority voting procedure was adopted. As one trade-union leader commented, however, these reforms did not transform the ETUC from ' "a coordination body between national centres" into a "transnational organisation". Clearly, not all ETUC affiliates, especially the largest among them, are ready to make this move.' (Visser and Ebbinghaus 1992, p. 223) While the labour movement weakens at the national level, conditions at the European level do not favour more effective forms of union organisation there (p. 236).

Environmental groups have also faced problems in organising at the European level. Despite 6.5 million ECU spent in 1992 on non-governmental environmental groups by DG XI (Rucht 1993, p. 87), the groups lack resources. The principal environmental organisation, the European Environmental Bureau (EEB), had only three to four full-time staff members in 1992 (Rucht 1993, p. 83). In contrast, CEFIC alone had a staff of 80 and 4,000 company representatives involved in its committee work. The environmental groups have also been split by their objectives (which vary from broad ecological concerns to the protection of a particular species) and their methods of achieving them (which may range from informed and expert lobbying to illegal forms of direct action). A rival organisation to EEB is CEAT (Coordination Européenne des Amis de la Terre) which was set up in 1985 by Friends of the Earth and takes only one member organisation from each country covered. 'As a rule, CEAT groups tend to be more conflict-oriented and have a stronger orientation towards grass-roots groups than most of those represented in the EEB.' (Rucht 1993, p. 84) In short, there is one organisation for insider groups and another for those with more of an outsider orientation.

Rucht (1993, pp. 87–9) summarises the weakness of the environmental groups in terms of the following factors:

1. A dependence on EC subsidies which may undermine their autonomy.
2. Lack of homogeneity. Structural and ideological diversity makes it difficult to agree on common positions and strategies.
3. Lack of institutional access.

4. Their reactive character, responding to an agenda set by the Commission which is not generally dependent on public opinion.

5. Strong opponents in a number of industrial sectors.

Mazey and Richardson (1992b), in contrast, develop an analysis which emphasises what they see as the strengths of environmental groups operating at a European level. Their strongest argument is that 'The ability of environmental groups to set the political agenda is perceived by the industrialists to whom we have spoken as perhaps the greatest current asset of the environmentalists.' (p. 120) They claim that 'The European level environmental groups may seem quite well resourced when compared with sectoral business associations at the European level.' (p. 122) They compare Greenpeace, with twelve full-time staff in its Brussels office, with the European Association of Textile Polyolefins (EATP), with only four. This is not really a very useful comparison as EATP is a product association, or at best a subsectoral association, rather than a sectoral association such as CEFIC. Indeed, they go on to admit 'that in those areas of environmental policy where industry has a really keen and vital interest, the resources mobilised are very considerable indeed and usually far outweigh those of any of the environmental groups' (p. 123). They concede that environmental groups are over-reliant on links with DG XI, and they also point out that industrial interests are mobilising more effectively in relation to the environmental issue, although whether being 'proactive' rather than 'reactive' in lobbying style is as big an asset as Mazey and Richardson claim depends on how accurately and how far one can anticipate the future.

The environmental groups which have been most successful at the European level tend to be well-resourced organisations with clear objectives arising from a very specific focus. The best-resourced British environmental group, the RSPB, 'was closely involved with the European Commission in the formulation of the EC Directive on the Conservation of Wild Birds and Zoo Check was partly sponsored by the EC to undertake a study of European zoos which has resulted in a proposed directive to impose uniform standards' (Garner 1993, pp. 190–1).

The only interests that are of rival importance to business in terms of resources are the territorial interests, with around one hundred regions represented in Brussels. Like business, these often have the advantage of organising institutions rather than individuals (Salisbury 1984), often regional governments. The author received an invitation to visit the 'embassy' of a German Land in Brussels. It is not surprising that the opening of a regional Brussels office often alarms national governments (Mazey and Mitchell 1993). These efforts, however, often disappoint their sponsors. For example, there is reason to believe that the Welsh strategy of 'by-passing London' and going straight to Brussels has yielded less results than was hoped for.

However, the increasing emphasis on regions in the European Union, with the Committee of the Regions being established by the Maastricht treaty, does mean that regional interests are likely to be increasingly emphasised. There is, however, still a long way to go before there is a 'transformation of national into regional economies and of sub-national regions into subunits of a supranational economy [amounting] to a *regionalization of Europe* as well as at the same time a *Europeanization of its regions*' (Streeck and Schmitter 1991, p. 153). The regional interests are not really a counterpart to business interests, in the sense that trade-union, consumer or environmental interests could be. Indeed, the regional interests are to some extent competing with each other for a share of foreign direct investment, and for aid to construct infrastructure that will make their regions more attractive to business investors. Their activities are not in competition with those of business, and in some respects are complementary to them.

Outsider groups can take their own initiatives to improve their position. Having used the European Parliament to forestall a proposed directive to ban 'big bikes', the Motorcycle Action Group entered into merger discussions with the rival British Motorcycle Federation. This somewhat contentious step was taken because 'we want the riders' movement in the UK and Europe to be in the best possible position to fight the coming battles on the EC Directive' (Statement by MAG National Chairman, March 1994). Other groups need to make more effort to join MAG on their ride into Europe.

European corporatism?

There has always been something of an ideological predisposition towards corporatism in the European Commission. In part, this is because many of the member states have Christian and social democratic traditions which have made them well disposed to corporatism. It is also because corporatist arrangements have been perceived as one way of assisting the integration process. In the jargon of the Union, the terms used have been 'social partnership' and 'social dialogue'. In the 1970s there was a Bureau of Social Partners – not a marriage agency, but an attempt to involve the trade unions more effectively in the work of the European institutions.

In the 1970s social partnership was promoted through a series of 'Tripartite Conferences' which came to an end in 1978 after the ETUC withdrew because so little was being achieved. They were revived in 1985 through meetings at the Val Duchesse castle near Brussels involving members of the commission headed by Jacques Delors, UNICE, the ETUC, and the European Centre for Public Enterprises (CEEP). In 1989, a political-level steering group was set up to develop the social dialogue, with priority being given to education and training and labour-market issues. The employers gave rather reluctant assent to this process. According to the head of the CBI Brussels office:

> It is worth stressing that we see UNICE as our lobby and no more than our lobby. Three years ago we stretched a point and agreed that it should become our social partner, i.e. that it should meet in joint session with the European TUC, under Commission chairmanship and should develop the social dialogue.
>
> (Eberlie 1993, p. 204)

Article 118b of the Single European Act gave a formal status to the notion of social dialogue, stating, 'The Commission shall endeavour to develop the dialogue between management and labour at European level which could, if the two sides consider it desirable, lead to relations based on agreement.' This idea was extended in the agreement on social policy in the Maastricht treaty – which was not signed by Britain. The CBI had initially agreed to support the proposal after it had found itself in a minority of one in UNICE, but backed down after opposition from within its membership to any notion of binding implementation (Grant 1993a, p. 190).

The agreement on social policy in the Maastricht treaty establishes 'dialogue between management and labour' as one of the objectives to be pursued in the implementation of the 1989 Social Charter. The implementation of directives in areas such as social security, redundancy protection and employee representation may be entrusted by a member state to management and labour at their joint request, a classic neo-corporatist provision. Article 4 of the agreement provides for management and labour to arrive at agreements which can then be implemented by a Council decision.

Attempts to arrive at an agreement between UNICE and the ETUC on works councils broke down in March 1994 after months of discussion, leaving the Council of Ministers to pass a directive. It had been hoped that an agreement between the social partners would be possible after UNICE moved towards the ETUC position by accepting the principle of a legal right to information for employees. The ETUC complained that the withdrawal of the CBI from the negotiations had undermined UNICE's authority. The CBI was unhappy about earlier concessions made by UNICE (*Financial Times*, 31 March 1994).

These developments fit in with Streeck and Schmitter's conclusion (1991, p. 156):

> Tripartism never really worked in Brussels, and where it was tried, it was always too encapsulated and marginal to come in any way close to a neocorporatist mode of governance. There is no reason to believe this will change.

Tripartism was, of course, in part an effort to create institutional mechanisms to ensure that business interests were counterbalanced by organised labour. In the closing years of the twentieth century, the conflict between capital and labour represented by the politics of production is no longer at centre stage, and there has been a shift towards a politics of collective consumption (Grant 1993a). The task for the European Union is to ensure that less-organised interests such as consumers, environmentalists, women and the elderly are able to make their voices heard in European institutions alongside that of business. As migration, asylum and freedom-of-movement issues become the subject of agreement between member states, even if outside the Community institutions through intergovernmental agreements such as Shengen and the Dublin Convention (Malhan 1994), more effective ways of involving the Union's many ethnic minorities in its decision-making will have to be found. Even the riders of large motor bikes should be inside the building talking to officials rather than on the road outside on their annual Euro Demo.

Broadening the interest base is not a straightforward matter, as many of these interests are deeply divided in terms of their goals. For example, devout Catholic women usually have a different perspective on family issues from feminists. The consumer 'interest' is notoriously difficult to organise because those who speak for it may represent a subset of the middle class for whom quality issues are paramount, while the less well-off may be more concerned about price. Consumer organisations are not as developed in Southern Europe as in Northern Europe. Of the various organisations represented in the Bureau Européen des Unions de Consommateurs (BEUC), only four (including the Consumers' Association in Britain) can claim to be independent of government in the sense that they receive no government funding.

If the new Europe is to be characterised by more than 'disjointed pluralism' or 'competitive federalism' (Streeck and Schmitter 1991, p. 157), the European institutions will have to play a greater role in steering the development of interest organisations. All that seems to be on offer at the moment, however, is a regulation of lobbyists which may enhance their importance without effectively controlling them, and a reinforcement of the insider–outsider distinction, leading to 'the emergence of an "inner" and "outer" circle of Eurogroups' (Mazey and Richardson 1993a, p. 22). While such a development might lighten 'lobbying overload', it might be less beneficial for democracy because it could reinforce the existing biases which tend to favour big, multinational business.

7

The effectiveness of pressure groups

Any study of pressure groups must be concerned not only with how they operate, but also with what they are able to achieve. Questions about who gains and who loses should be at the core of any political analysis. Difficult methodological problems arise, however, in the analysis of effectiveness. What is the pattern of cause and effect? Do groups become more effective because government policy changes in a way that makes them of central importance, as can be argued to have happened with the National Farmers' Union after the passage of the 1947 Agriculture Act? Similarly, in relation to overseas aid policy, 'the relative success enjoyed by business interests in winning concessions from the government owes as much to the reorientation of aid policy as to the skill and influence of the lobby itself' (Bose 1991, p. 143). Recent writing has challenged accounts of pressure-group capture of government and argued that 'State actors have incorporated groups in order to achieve their own goals.' (Smith 1993, p. 228) Are groups responding to an agenda and policy opportunities created by government, or do groups themselves bring about changes in government policy which in turn give them new opportunities to exert influence?

In 1994 the Conservative Government announced a 15 per cent cut in its road-building programme. Did this indicate that the Government was at last responding to the growing volume of protests against new roads which united local residents with travelling activists? Or was it a belated recognition of the fact that building new roads stimulates additional traffic demand, because people make journeys they wouldn't have made before when they were more time-consuming? The first question points to a response in terms of pressure politics, the second to the potential influence of an informed debate about the limitations of existing policy.

In any case, most environmental groups thought that the cuts were what Transport 2000 described as a 'con', leaving in place most of the schemes viewed as environmentally damaging. The Road Haulage Association described the cuts as 'less severe than expected', while the Federation of Civil Engineering Contractors said, 'it could have been a lot worse' (*Financial Times*, 31 March 1994). Almost immediately, the Government found itself faced with a new round of direct action against a by-pass round Bath, although on this occasion residents in one of the villages afflicted by existing traffic demonstrated in favour of the new road.

In 1993 environmentalists and local people had secured the withdrawal of a major road scheme in London which would have cut a swathe through Oxleas Wood, an ancient woodland and green lung on Shooters Hill in south-east London. However, by the time the project was withdrawn, no one was in favour of it, even the roads lobby. Winning a particular battle, however worthwhile, may distract attention from the failure to win the wider war. There seems little doubt, however, that demonstrations against controversial road-building projects, whether on Twyford Down or in east London, will continue, increasing costs for contractors. These efforts may be effective only in the long run, possibly after the election of a new government which gives a higher priority to public transport, although this observation, of itself, suggests that there are limits to the pressure-group approach to securing policy change. Moreover, any government has to be conscious of the large number of voters who are also motorists, many of whom consider that they have a right to drive where they like, when they like and, in some cases, how they like.

Even a brief consideration of the example of protests against road-building suggests that policy changes may be dependent on a number of factors, which include the following:

1. The salience of the issue to the electorate.
2. The political outlook of the government in office.

3. Expert 'scientific' opinion on the subject.
4. The balance of pressure-group activity.

Despite its importance, Whiteley and Winyard (1987, p. 111) note that 'the question of interest group effectiveness is probably the least adequately researched aspect of the study of pressure groups'. This may be because such an analysis can raise as many questions as it answers, although that of itself can be worthwhile. The underlying problem is the difficulties that arise in the analysis of two concepts which are at the centre of the study of politics: power and influence.

Indeed, the existence of two distinct terms – power and influence – itself hints at some of the problems. Without going into a complex conceptual debate, power may be said to refer to the exercise of authority ('legitimate power') by government and the deployment of coercive power by a non-governmental authority (such as a trade union). Both senses embody in them the notion of 'command', of obedience because one party either ought to be obeyed or has the ability to force the other party to obey. Influence, on the other hand, rests on the power to persuade, and is the most usual way in which pressure groups are able to affect the decision-making process. Government makes concessions to a pressure group because of the validity of its arguments, for example because the group is able to demonstrate that the proposed policy is unworkable or would damage the economy, or because its arguments have moral force. Government and Parliament may also be influenced by the state of public opinion on the particular issue, although it must be stressed that the majority of issues discussed between pressure groups and government are of such a technical character that there is no public opinion in relation to them.

Why measuring pressure-group influence is difficult

Even if the British political process were conducted in conditions of less secrecy, it would be difficult to estimate the effectiveness of a pressure group. The first problem arises from the objectives of the group itself. Some cause groups have relatively simple objectives, and it is possible to say whether or not they have been attained. Thus, those who campaigned for the release of the Beirut hostage, John McCarthy, eventually achieved their objective and the organisation was dissolved. If all blood sports were banned, the role of organisations opposing them might be limited to helping to ensure that they did not take place illegally. Most cause groups, however, have multiple objectives.

Matters become much more difficult when one considers sectional groups. Such groups invariably have multiple objectives. Some of these objectives may matter a great deal to them, others much less so. Indeed, the complex internal politics of such groups may lead to policies being developed which are intended to appease some faction or interest within the group, but which are not really supported by the leadership. Obviously, such policies will not be pressed very hard. Even supposing, however, that it were possible to attach weights to the various policies being advocated by a group, one would still be left with the problem of measuring the degree of success attained.

Occasionally, a sectional group gets all that it wants on a particular issue. For much of the time, however, it has to agree to a compromise. The compromise may be a bad one from the group's point of view, yet the group leadership may put a gloss on it to calm the membership. Equally, the compromise may be quite a favourable one, but the group may still complain loudly about the harshness of its treatment, largely for the consumption of its membership. Even trying to trace the real impact of the compromise on the group's members may be very difficult, as much will depend on its implementation. There are many provisions on the statute book which are hardly ever used.

There are also problems in deciding what government's priorities really are. Sometimes government may toughen up a Green Paper or a White Paper so that it has something to give away to pressure groups at a later stage without compromising its core position. In other cases, issuing a Green Paper may be interpreted as a sign that the Cabinet is internally divided, and that the government's commitment to any particular outcome is limited. For example, the decision to issue a Green Paper on the proposed sale of 51 per cent of the Royal Mail and Parcelforce was interpreted as a sign of uncertainty about whether the policy could be secured in the face of back-bench opposition: 'in issuing a consultative document ministers were acknowledging that they may have to dilute their sell-off option or even drop it' (*Financial Times*, 30 May 1994). Policy also often emerges as a series of compromises produced on the basis of interdepartmental arguments, with each department frequently arguing for the client groups with which it is associated.

In any case, how does one compare a substantial impact on a policy which is basically unfavourable to a group with some small adjustments to a policy which is more in line with a group's thinking? This is not a purely academic issue. The CBI had much more influence on the policy of the Labour Government of 1974–9 than it did on the policies of the preceding and succeeding Conservative governments. However, the policy proposals of the Labour Government were potentially more threatening to the CBI's interests than those of the Conservatives. The position is further complicated by the fact that members of the Labour Government were either opposed to particular policies (substantial intervention in industry) or unenthusiastic about them (industrial democracy). Hence, the CBI was a useful ally for the more moderate members of the Government in their internal policy struggles.

If one considers the interaction between pressure groups and government, it is relatively rare for only one group to be active on a particular issue. A number of groups will be taking a variety of positions, and using different strategies. In some cases, they may have allies in government departments. For example, Alarm UK, which coordinates 250 anti-road groups, claimed that the cut-back in road-building projects was partly due to a broad and growing opposition movement, but added, 'We can't take all the credit because the Treasury and the Environment department are also applying pressure.' (The *Independent*, 27 April 1994)

Whiteley and Winyard (1987, p. 111) suggest that 'a second-best solution to observing the decision-making process directly' is to interview participants and obtain their perceptions of effectiveness. Much useful data can be obtained in this way, although large-scale studies of this kind, such as have been carried out in the United States, are expensive and would need to be repeated from time to time to capture changing perceptions. In the rest of this chapter, an attempt is made to isolate the more important factors which might affect the effectiveness of a pressure group.

A typology of factors affecting pressure-group effectiveness

The following typology draws on a number of sources in the pressure-group literature. Among the most influential have been Presthus (1973, 1974); Schmitter and Streeck (1981), and the literature of the Organisation of Business Interests project in general; Whiteley and Winyard (1987); and the work of the Aberdeen group (for example Jordan 1994).

The typology is divided into three main categories which are then subdivided into subsidiary headings:

1. Features of the proximate environment of groups, the domains they are seeking to organise. In particular:
    (i) the characteristics of the potential membership being organised or represented;
    (ii) competition between groups for members and influence.
2. The resources available to groups:
    (i) internal group structures such as decision-taking and conflict-reduction mechanisms;
    (ii) marketing skills in terms of the attraction and retention of members;
    (iii) membership mobilisation capabilities;
    (iv) financial resources;
    (v) staffing resources;
    (vi) sanctioning capability;
    (vii) choices of strategy.
3. Features of the external economic and political environment:
    (i) public opinion/attitudes;
    (ii) the political party in office;
    (iii) economic circumstances, especially in relation to public expenditure;
    (iv) sponsorship or support by a government department, and/or opposition by other departments;
    (v) delegated authority.

The rest of the chapter will be structured around a consideration of these various points.

Domain organisation

Schmitter and Streeck (1981, pp. 146–7) observe the following:

> The most basic decision in the design of an interest association is to select from the variety of existing interests those which the association will represent, and to institutionalize a distinction between these and other interests whose representation is left to other associations. Interest associations define the interests they choose to internalize by formally demarcating an organizational domain.

In other words, pressure groups will decide whom it is they are seeking to represent, and this decision will be reflected in criteria of membership eligibility set out in their constitution. Of course, membership of some cause groups is open to the population at large. For all sectional groups, however, membership is limited in some way. Among cause groups, some may draw their members from a particular disadvantaged category, while others may be made up of concerned individuals seeking to remedy the problems of those in the disadvantaged category. Whiteley and Winyard (1987, p. 27) formalise this distinction, considering promotional groups as those 'that speak on behalf of, or *for* the poor, while representational groups are those whose membership is made up *of* the poor, or a particular category of claimant'.

Interestingly, Whiteley and Winyard found that, if anything, the promotional groups were more effective than the representational groups. This appeared to be because the representational groups were not seen by civil servants as truly representative of their categories, or able to deliver their clienteles, while the promotional groups displayed more professional expertise in pressure-group activity (pp. 132–3). Another relevant factor appeared to be the 'attractiveness' of the client group in terms of its electoral influence and the degree to which it was seen as 'deserving'. It is easier to arouse public concern and the support of decision-makers for the elderly than for, say, offenders or the low paid (p. 131).

It is important for a group with a restricted eligible membership to organise as large a proportion of it as possible in order to be credible. Trade associations will often claim with pride that they represent 93 per cent of the firms in terms of sales or employment in the widget industry or whatever sector they are organising. Indeed, Presthus (1974, p. 111) argues that 'size and quality of membership are probably among the major political resources of interest groups'. Cause groups in Britain tend to attract a disproportionate number of well-educated, middle-class members. The Aberdeen group's data show that 35.3 per cent of Friends of the Earth members had a first degree, 18.9 per cent held a postgraduate degree, and 10 per cent were still in higher education, making a total of 64 per cent of members with a high level of education (Jordan 1994, Table 7). Such individuals tend to have high levels of self-confidence and to be articulate, good at drafting papers, knowledgeable about the political system and able to hold their own in meetings with officials.

In practice, there is considerable overlap between the domains of pressure groups. Sometimes, this overlap is accidental. For example, the structure of trade associations in Britain has grown on an *ad hoc* basis over a hundred years or so, and is consequently beset by a lack of coherence in the division of responsibilities. Sometimes, however, overlaps may reflect differences of interest. For example, the construction industry has a large number of associations representing, for example, large firms and small firms, contractors and subcontractors, civil engineers and builders, etc. To some extent, each of these associations could be said to be representing distinct domains. However, it is clear that some of the associations are competing for members and influence, leading to a situation in which government has a series of voices claiming to speak for the industry. West Germany has had a much more coherent structure of associations in the industry (see Grant and Streeck 1985). Against the background of the Heseltine initiative to encourage the development of one leading business association in each sector, the formation of an umbrella group for the construction industry was announced in June 1994 (*Financial Times*, 2 June 1994).

Such competition for members and influence is not limited to sectional groups. Cause groups may be divided along such lines as the tactics to be used to further a shared objective, as, for example, with the anti-hunting lobby. In the disability field, 'There has been considerable rivalry between the Disablement Income Group, the Royal Association for Disability and Rehabilitation and the Disability Alliance' (Whiteley and Winyard 1987, p. 134). As existing organisations concerned with the elderly moved towards greater consensus in the mid-1980s, they found themselves faced with a new wave of group formation, in part stimulated by the availability of funding from local councils. 'These fledgling groups were indicative of a grass roots upsurge, to which the more- established pensioner organizations now struggled to respond.' (Pratt 1993, p. 143)

If groups representing a potentially homogeneous category of interest are divided, then government has the option of using a 'divide and rule' strategy. In the dispute about new contracts in further education colleges in 1994, the National Association of Teachers in Further and Higher Education (NATFHE), the main union, made use of the strike weapon, leading some members to leave and join the more moderate Association of Teachers and Lecturers (ATL) which emphasised negotiations. However, even leaving aside ideologically based disagreements about strategies and tactics, it is not necessarily easy for groups to get together and present a united front. A merger or joint action may be more in the interests of one group than another. Teaching unions have been particularly prone to competition for members and influence, but Coates makes it clear in his study of the teaching unions that the National Union of Teachers (NUT) had the most to gain from organisational unity:

> The impetus for the creation of a single teachers' organisation has come always from the largest association, the NUT . . . . Lack of unity, in the Union's view, dissipated the potential for influence that the teachers collectively possessed through the traditional forms of their pressure. And, of course, as the largest of the associations by far, the NUT had the most to gain from the creation of an organisational unit that it would inevitably dominate, and in which sectional voices would be muted.
>
> (Coates 1972, p. 47)

It is not surprising that, over twenty years later, the teaching unions remain divided, with one new organisation being added to the total, the anti-strike Professional Association of Teachers.

Equally, it is clear that, where pressure groups have been able to supplant competitors, this has been an important source of strength. Before the Second World War, 'the influence of farmers on agricultural policy was not strong', one reason being that 'In the thirties the NFU was only one of several agricultural pressure groups trying to influence Government' (Smith 1988, p. 5). The leading position of the NFU in the agricultural policy community is in part a reflection of its success 'at accommodating the conflicts between the various branches of farming to create a single "farmers' view" ' (Smith 1993, p. 105).

Resources: internal group structures

One of the ways in which the NFU has reduced external competition is by having an internal structure in which a variety of viewpoints (according to different commodities, different types of land, etc.) can be fed into the organisation's decision-making process. Similar devices are employed by many trade associations, for example special committees or reserved seats on the main decision-making body for small-firm members who may otherwise feel excluded by larger members.

Despite the usefulness of devices of this kind, there is a difficult trade-off between a widely based organisation with a large membership but significant internal tensions, and an organisation with a small, but tightly knit membership. It is sometimes said, for instance, that the CBI suffers from 'stifling breadth' because it attempts to represent small and large firms; manufacturers, financiers and retailers; nationalised industries and private-sector firms; importers and exporters, etc. Indeed, concern that the CBI failed to articulate sufficiently clearly the distinctive concerns of manufacturing industry led to the formation of new organisations in the 1990s. The UK Industrial Group organised seventy companies with a turnover of £1.5 billion with a call for an end to the decline in the nation's manufacturing base. The British Management Data Foundation had a similar aim of winning better support for manufacturing and organised 21 major companies such as Allied-Lyons, ICI, Marks and Spencer and Shell UK. Its director argued that it was 'less unwieldy than a group such as the [CBI] which represents hundreds of companies' (*Financial Times*, 19 January 1992). This group held meetings with the Prime Minister's press secretary. In 1993 Michael Heseltine set up his own network of contacts with around twenty leading industrialists. This group, which met for dinner at Lancaster House in London, included the chairmen or chief executives of National Westminster Bank, TI Engineering, Sainsbury's, Unigate Foods and Mercury Communications.

It is clear that 'A central problem in the design of associational structures is the management of internal interest diversity' (Schmitter and Streeck 1981, p. 142). Highly publicised exits of members (as has happened in the CBI) and the formation of breakaway organisations (as has happened in the CBI and NFU) can be damaging to an organisation's reputation. On the other hand, the price of preventing such splits may be a high one in terms of the quality of the policies produced and their impact on government.

Pressure groups have to develop decision-making structures which take account of the different interests and viewpoints of their members whilst being able to develop effective policies and to respond to changing events. In many sectional groups, a typical pattern is to have a large council which is the ultimate decision-making body but which only really takes decisions in situations where significant sections of the membership are offended by a policy proposal. An executive committee is often in effective charge of the overall strategy of the organisation. Much of the real work, however, is done by a series of specialised committees dealing with particular problem areas. These may, in turn, spawn working parties to deal with a particular piece of legislation or EU directive. Coordinating the work of these various committees, and keeping the overall committee structure under review, is one of the tasks of the professional staffs of the associations.

Cause groups vary in their structures from being hierarchical and centralised to democratic and decentralised. In general, however, they have less elaborate organisational charts (if they have one at all) compared with the larger sectional groups. Many cause groups have a relatively decentralised structure, often for ideological reasons. Such structures have their advantages and disadvantages. They involve members in local protest actions which are often seen by cause groups as an important part of their work. They can feed back information on how government policies are working in practice on the ground. Whiteley and Winyard's research shows that civil servants valued information from pressure groups on how the social security system was working in practice so that shortcomings could be identified and rectified (1987, pp. 131–2). On the other hand, a decentralised structure may lead to local groups taking actions which contradict group policy or embarrass the group and make its relations with civil servants more difficult. In a decentralised organisation, the centre may be starved of the financial resources it requires to function effectively.

This helps to explain why groups such as Greenpeace have opted for hierarchical structures with little democratic control over the direction of campaigns:

Internally, Greenpeace has a strictly bureaucratic, if not author-
itarian, structure. A small group of people has control over the
organisation both at the international level and within national
chapters. Local action groups, which exist in some countries, are
totally dependent on the central body, and the rank and file is
excluded from all decisions.

(Rucht 1993, p. 85)

The Aberdeen group's research raises the general issue of
whether many cause groups are networks of financial supporters
rather than memberships. By subscribing one engages in a cultural
identification rather than in any form of political participation.
Mail-order membership means that 'For a cost that is not seriously
considered by the relatively affluent potential member, they can
make a political statement of preference without engaging in
"real" participation.' (Jordan 1994, p. 27) Following through the
logic of this argument, one might 'join' an environmental group in
the same way that one sends a donation to a charity: as a declara-
tion of support, but not in the expectation or hope of participating
in a decision-making process. This does not mean that democratic
decision-making structures within groups are always well used
where they exist. Members of the NFU do not flock to their branch
meetings, but the opportunity is there for them to participate in
the development of policy if they want to take it.

Marketing skills and membership mobilisation

The development by the Aberdeen group of a marketing perspective on pressure-group activities draws our attention to the extent
to which, in order to succeed, a cause group has to go out and sell a
'product' to a potential membership. Sectional groups are often in
a rather different position, because their members are either institutions which face a different calculus about the costs and benefits of membership, or, if they are individuals, membership may be
required for professional reasons. Dunleavy's work shows that 'endogenous groups . . . formed simply by the coming together of
like-minded people' (1991, p. 55) face a number of problems in
constructing group identities:

1. The identity set is diffuse, 'unrelated to any specific social
   situation or clear target profile' (p. 66).

2. The potential members are often socially invisible because they are distinguished by non-observable private mental states.
3. Identity sets are unstable with high turnover because one can change one's views more easily than a social role (such as an occupation).

Dunleavy goes on to draw out a number of second-order implications from these observations. In summary, endogenous groups have heterogeneous memberships in which the shared identity can be pursued by means other than collective action. Exit costs are low: they involve, at most, changing a preference (whereas leaving a professional group might involve leaving an occupation). There is likely to be group rivalry and high membership turnover, the latter prediction being confirmed by the Aberdeen group's data.

The Aberdeen group see 'the size of group membership as linked to the marketing strategies and success of the groups' (Jordan, Maloney and McLaughlin 1994b, p. 549). Thus, the conspicuous success of the RSPB 'reflects the success of regular and high profile press advertising and increased sophistication in recruitment rather than just a change in public attitudes' (p. 549). Anyone in the population can join the RSPB, although some members of the population have a strong attachment to a particular species (some very keen bird-watchers have a strong dislike of cats, some cat-lovers dislike dog owners, etc.). What is clear from the Aberdeen group's data is that there is a subset of the population who are 'joiners' (a term which had some currency in earlier empirical American sociological literature, but has been rather lost from view). Thus, 73.5 per cent of the members of Amnesty belong to another organisation, with the corresponding figure for members of Friends of the Earth being 65.8 per cent. Overlapping membership is particularly high between Amnesty and Friends of the Earth or Greenpeace (or both), but the Aberdeen group's sample contained 35 respondents who were members of both Amnesty and the RSPB.

In a society in which at least some people are affluent, the cost of multiple group membership is relatively low. Becoming an activist, however, incurs much higher costs. For example, an individual who becomes a hunt saboteur runs the risk of physical assault and prosecution. However, the identification involved in such a choice is far stronger than the person who sends off a cheque to the World Wide Fund for Nature and displays a sticker in their car. A hunt saboteur may well be involved in other forms of direct action on behalf of animals and their social life may be constructed around a group of animal activists.

Some groups depend more than others on their ability to mobilise their members. The CBI does not ask its members to take to the streets, but if a trade union makes a strike threat, it needs to be able to rely on the support of members in a postal ballot. Following Dunleavy (1991, p. 20), the actions which members are asked to perform on behalf of the group may be ranked from low cost to high cost, ranging from lobbying elected representatives, through demonstrations, to civil disobedience. Groups such as Amnesty International depend substantially on their individual members to engage in campaigns on behalf of individual prisoners who are 'adopted' by local branches.

Enthusiastic volunteer activists may, however, lack the detachment and balance of professional staff members, and create problems for a pressure group. Tensions may arise in organisations which have a small core of professional staff and a large number of volunteer activists. The activists may resent the fact that resources are being devoted to the payment of staff for activities which they undertake for free, while the staff may consider that the activists lack the professional approach that successful group activity requires.

Financial resources, staff size and sanctioning capacity

Financial resources are important to a group in the sense that if it is going to engage in the detailed monitoring of legislation, including EU directives, and attempt to influence the content of such legislation through the presentation of a detailed case to civil servants, it will require a large, relatively well-paid staff. As Moran (1983, p. 51) observes, 'The characteristic way in which powerful interests have influenced policy-making in modern Britain may be summarised in one word: they have done so *bureaucratically*.' Having interviewed many pressure-group officials over the years, one of the most striking characteristics of most of them is their similarity to civil servants in terms of their official personalities, modes of operation, language, and perceptions of the political process. After all, they *are* civil servants, preparing policy papers for and generally servicing committees, and making presentations to their counterparts in government. Such skills have to be developed by cause groups, just as much as by sectional groups, if they want to be effective. 'Insider access, indeed legitimacy, is granted to Amnesty because it provides the government with good information which can be used as a lever in international negotiations.' (Christiansen and Dowding 1994, p. 21)

Buksti and Johansen suggest on the basis of Danish research that the size of the secretariat or bureaucracy of an organisation is an important determinant of group effectiveness. They characterise organisations with fewer than six people on their staff as 'weak insiders' (1979, pp. 209–10). A rather similar view was taken by the Devlin Commission on Industrial Representation, which suggested that an effective association should have an executive staff of at least eight people.

This view does, however, need some qualification. For example, a product-level association which has to consider particular EU directives can operate quite effectively with a part-time executive officer shared with other similar associations and operating out of the offices of the sectoral association (a pattern adopted in the chemical and food-processing industries, for example). At the other end of the spectrum, there is a danger that a large association bureaucracy will develop objectives of its own which are at variance with those of the members. Indeed, one argument that has been put to me in an interview is that a small secretariat of a few very well-paid executives concentrating on major issues can work just as well as an association with large numbers of middle-ranking officials scrutinising the details of policy, although in practice such details can be very significant.

One also has to consider the calibre of the staff themselves. What qualities are required of pressure-group officials? Some associations like to recruit from the industry they represent, which may be sensible if the association's work has a substantial technical content. Occasionally, high-ranking civil servants nearing retirement are recruited to head an association on the realistic assumption that they will know their way around the corridors of Whitehall. Some associations like to recruit retired military personnel to staff their organisations, but in some cases this has had disastrous consequences, given that pressure groups are complex organisations which do not respond to instructions in the same way as military subordinates. An increasing trend in recent years has been the emergence of the pressure-group professional who is recognised as having a collection of skills which can be transferred from one organisation to another (this is particularly applicable to trade associations, but instances have also occurred among cause groups). However, there is no real profession of association management, as there is no real specialised training and no professional examinations.

For campaigning groups, the whole idea of professionalism may seem anathema, with career structures getting in the way of commitment and campaigning zeal. Unfortunately, a person who is good at running a campaign or thinking up a media stunt may not have the management skills necessary to run an office:

> This was a fundamental dilemma with which Greenpeace is still grappling today. Do you rely on well-meaning, highly motivated people working for an ideal rather than for money? Or do you recognise that the outfit is, to all intents and purposes, a multinational which needs professional skills at the highest level?
>
> (Wilkinson 1994, p. 42)

Financial resources are often important if a pressure group is to be influential in the long run, as distinct from having a one-off success resulting from riding a tide in public opinion. However, it should be noted that there are instances of pressure groups with small secretariats being influential, either because their cooperation was seen as important to the attainment of government policy objectives, or because they possessed resources of expertise among their members. The influence of the Round Table on EU policies is because of the importance of its members and the quality of their arguments, not the size of its secretariat.

There are instances where a group's influence may depend more on its sanctioning capacity than on the quality of its arguments. The most successful political strike in the post-war period was that coordinated by the Ulster Workers' Council which paralysed Northern Ireland for two weeks in May 1974, bringing down the 'power-sharing' executive after only five months in office. Although it achieved its immediate objective, it did nothing to solve Northern Ireland's problems, and may well have made them worse. The Conservative Governments after 1979 set out, with considerable success, to restrain the use of the strike weapon by trade unions. When the Government used state power to crush a number of strikes, notably that of the miners, in the 1980s, there was little reaction from the public at large, fed up with the inconvenience of the strikes of the 1970s. The unions devalued the strike weapon by its excessive and inappropriate use.

The City of London has considerable sanctioning capacity because it can engage in a 'gilt-edged strike' by refusing to buy government stock, or 'talk down' sterling because of unease about government policy. Because of the internationalisation of foreign exchange markets, however, sterling is more likely to be influenced by, for example, statements by the Bundesbank about the trend in interest rates. Movements in share prices in London are, however, extensively reported by the media, and can be interpreted as a verdict on government performance. A future Labour government would have to reassure the financial services market. Indeed, the Labour opposition made considerable efforts to do just that in the run-up to the 1992 election with some success. The need to take such action does suggest, however, that the financial markets exert a constraining influence over policy, with their message being reinforced when necessary by the Governor of the Bank of England in his regular (and now publicly minuted) meetings with the Chancellor. The sanctioning power of the financial services sector is not exerted through traditional pressure-group channels, although financial institutions use those as well.

The choice of strategy

The choice of an appropriate strategy and tactics can be an important determinant of pressure-group success, although there is a sense in which the adoption of unsophisticated strategies may be a reflection of ineffectiveness rather than its cause. Whiteley and Winyard (1987, p. 136) conclude:

> A quiet insider strategy does not pay off any better than an open promotional strategy. Since the era of consensus politics described by Beer and Eckstein, policy making has become more conflictual, but also more fragmented.

Whiteley and Winyard's research shows that the responsible use of publicity by a group can reinforce the lobbying of government. It is also apparent that there are more opportunities for exerting influence through Parliament than was the case in the 1950s when the first empirical pressure-group studies were undertaken. Even so, it is clear that much success in lobbying still depends on the careful research and analysis of a case, and its presentation to civil servants. In that sense, the lobbying process remains a highly bureaucratised one in which adequate resources are one of the keys to success.

The Ramblers' Association has been striving to modify its image so that it can seek a new accommodation with landowners to secure the passage of a right-of-access bill through Parliament. The Association published a new discussion document which 'tries to live down the image of the rambler-activist, beard bristling with indignation' which was seen as 'counter-productive in gaining access to the countryside. It antagonises landowners [but also] upsets many ramblers.' (The *Independent*, 11 February 1993) The new approach, however, received an initially discouraging response from the Country Landowners' Association which dislikes the idea of *rights* for ramblers, believing that they could be misused by an irresponsible minority.

Frustration at the lack of success of 'responsible' strategies has increasingly led activists opposed to animal experiments or new roads to resort to direct action, where the principal objective is not to change government policy but to harm the economic interests of, for example, pharmaceutical or cosmetics companies or construction firms. Democracy can never promise that everyone gets what they want, and with new road schemes decision-making involves a difficult balancing act between conflicting interests. Such activists would doubtless object that the conventional political process is biased in favour of established interests. A more telling criticism is that direct action may undermine attempts to influence public opinion and change public policy, although, as Garner goes on to point out, much depends on the form of direct action used:

> The media emphasis on the extreme forms of direct action, it is argued, discredits the whole of the movement since the more moderate groups are tarred with the same brush. In addition, attention is diverted away from the issues on to the nature of the activities themselves – their threat to public safety and what can be done to stop them.
>
> (Garner 1993, p. 225)

One of the most conspicuous examples of the apparent success of an outsider strategy is the anti-poll tax movement. Considerable and successful use was made of non-payment as a tactic, sub-sequently developed into resistance against bailiffs, while a demonstration at Trafalgar Square developed into a serious riot. Non-payment was a particularly effective tactic because 'It tapped into a . . . tradition of civil disobedience going back into British history. It had the rare advantage of combining strong moral anger with material self-interest.' (Barr 1992, p. 145) Barr argues (p. 145) that non-payment was 'the winning strategy', but one also has to take into account how far the decision to abandon the tax was taken simply because Conservative MPs in marginal constituencies were afraid of losing their seats. It is doubtful whether the Conservatives could have won the 1992 election without abandoning the poll tax, although under-registration as a consequence of avoidance of the tax may have helped them to win. Barr concludes (p. 147) that 'The anti-poll tax movement has shown that outsider status and a total lack of interest in negotiation at the national level are not neces-sarily handicaps.' Certainly, it reminds us that outsider strategies can help to bring results, although refusals to pay tax have not usually been effective, and in this case were assisted by a widely shared sense that the poll tax was inherently unfair. Insider strategies are likely to be those pursued by the majority of pressure groups seek-ing to influence government policy.

External environment

Public attitudes and opinions are an important feature of the exter-nal operating environment of groups. A pressure group will usu-ally try and influence public opinion. Although such efforts may have some success, groups are more likely to benefit from a change in public views which they have not themselves brought about. An important distinction can be made between 'attitudes' and 'opin-ions'. It will not be possible to discuss the literature on this subject here. For the purposes of this analysis, attitudes are taken to refer to more deeply held perceptions which structure the response of individuals to particular events. They generally change only either slowly or in response to some crisis situation. Opinions are more superficial; they may reflect more deeply held attitudes, but they may also be more spontaneous responses to particular events.

As Richard Rose (1974, p. 253) points out, 'The likelihood of any group gaining wide popular support for its demands depends upon the congruence between group demands and the values, beliefs and emotions widely diffused in the culture.' Rose (pp. 254–5) develops a sixfold typology based on the level of congruence between a group's goals and wider cultural norms, which is presented here with updated examples:

1. 'Harmony between pressure group demands and general cultural norms.' Organisations opposing cruelty to children and to animals are clear examples.
2. 'A gradual increase in the acceptability of political values supporting pressure group demands.' Anti-smoking groups were once regarded as marginal organisations, but their demands now occupy a central position on the political agenda, although more so in the United States than in Britain.
3. 'Bargaining with fluctuating support from cultural norms.' An organisation like the CPRE may be seen as drawing on essential values of 'Englishness', but its concern about intensive leisure uses of the countryside would win support from some segments of the population, but not from others.
4. 'Advocacy in the face of cultural indifference.' Such a group lacks an audience either in government or outside it. The Pedestrians' Association has less than a thousand members compared with over seven million members in the AA.
5. 'Advocacy in opposition to long-term cultural trends.' Despite some victories, the advocates of restricted shop opening on Sundays have found it difficult to stem the combined effect of commercial pressures from retailers and apparent consumer preferences.
6. 'Conflict between cultural values and pressure group goals.' Apart from the Campaign for the Abolition of Angling, animal protection groups 'have fought shy of criticising angling because it is an extremely popular pastime and also because it is much more difficult to establish that fish can suffer' (Garner 1993, p. 172).

The importance of public opinion in setting a context for pressure-group activity can be seen by the way in which the environmental movement gained ground in the 1970s and 1980s, but then started to lose some ground in the early 1990s. *Social* groups between 1992 and 1993. A number of environmental groups had to cut staff because of falling income in the early 1990s. World Wide Fund for Nature lost £3 million in income between 1989 and 1992 and shed 20 jobs (10 per cent of its staff) in 1992, and another five jobs in 1993. Friends of the Earth made 24 of its 120 staff redundant in 1993. In part, the decline in income was a result of the recession – which also affected charitable giving – but it also reflected a growth of 'doom fatigue' among the public (*The Observer*, 27 June 1993).

Even before this fall-off in support – which could turn out to be a short-term phenomenon – there was a risk associated with the increased issue salience of environmentalism. First, 'many campaigns of the environmental groups remain issue-specific, tending to fade away in true "issue-attention" style . . . many groups still lack adequate resources to pursue and co-ordinate the campaigns they would like' (Robinson 1992, p. 98). Second, politicians may be tempted to jump on the bandwagon and make tokenistic commitments to the environmentalist cause. 'The main political parties are still chained to the idea that the natural ecosystem primarily exists as a resource for man's exploitation.' (Robinson 1992, p. 217)

Changes and continuities: parties and departments

The party in office can make a considerable difference to the political influence exerted by a pressure group. It must be emphasised that two governments with the same party label can be very different in their approach to pressure-group activity. The Heath Government tried to develop a close working relationship with the trade unions, while the Thatcher Government was keen to distance itself from them.

The TUC was the pressure group most adversely affected by the advent of the Thatcher Government. Using detailed data from TUC annual reports, Mitchell (1987) shows that the number of contacts at prime-ministerial level fell off sharply after 1979, although ministerial contacts remained at the same level as under the Labour Government of 1974–9. What changed even more dramatically was the effectiveness of contacts as perceived by the TUC. Between 1976 and 1979, the success rate in terms of government agreeing to take the action advocated by the TUC varied ment agreeing to take the action advocated by the TUC varied between 40.5 per cent and 47.0 per cent. In the years from 1979 to 1984, it ranges between 4.5 per cent and 22.5 per cent, a striking contrast with the earlier period. In 1992 it was announced that in the context of membership losses of four million from a 1979 figure of over 12 million, the TUC staff of 250 would have to be cut by up to a fifth (*Financial Times*, 24 February 1992).

The poverty lobby was also adversely affected by the political climate of the 1980s. 'In the Thatcherite era of conviction politics the influence of poverty groups has been reduced by the ideological beliefs of that administration, and by the deteriorating economic climate that monetarist policies have created' (Whiteley and Winyard 1987, p. 138). A lobby of a very different kind, the British Medical Association, was singled out in both Mrs Thatcher's and Nigel Lawson's memoirs for campaigning against government policy. Smith (1993, p. 183) brings out both the extent and the limits of the changes brought about in the nature of the health policy community:

> The government has attacked the consensus and ideology of the policy community by questioning clinical autonomy and removing the doctors' veto over both questions of implementation and wider policy. Consequently, conflict and new groups have . . . undermined the closed policy community that previously existed . . . . Doctors are still important to the process of making and implementing policy, and the structures of institutionalised access still exist.

In noting the changes brought about by the experience of Thatcherism, it is easy to ignore the continuities. Mrs Thatcher was reluctant to make changes in the structure of government (John Major created a new National Heritage department) and, if anything, the issue communities organised around government departments became more solidified in the 1980s. One of the key and enduring features of the British political process is the symbiotic relationship between groups and departments. The groups need the departments for access, status and information about policy developments; the departments need the groups for information about what is happening in their sphere of interest, for cooperation in the implementation of policy and, above all, as allies in the interdepartmental battles which are another key feature of the British political process. As new ministerial responsibilities emerge, new alliances are developed. Thus, when William

Waldegrave was green minister, the environmental groups 'were only too happy to play along with the game which he invited them to join, enlisting them as supporters of the department in the battles which they had to fight against other Government departments, particularly the Ministry of Agriculture' (Porritt and Winner 1988, p. 85).

The NFU has benefited considerably from being the only industry to have its own department in Whitehall (MAFF) with which it has close and well-developed links, even if the circle of consultation has been widened in recent years. Merging MAFF with the Department of the Environment, or even reorganising it as a Department of Rural Affairs, would restructure the policy community in a way which would undermine the NFU's position. Similarly, the abolition of sponsorship divisions for particular industries within the DTI, and their subsequent restoration by Michael Heseltine, significantly affected the policy map for industrial interests. It was probably, however, the small and weaker trade associations that relied most on the sponsorship divisions, and Heseltine's professed intention was to encourage trade association rationalisation by dealing principally with one organisation from each sector.

Support from a particular government department may always be offset by opposition from another department with different priorities (e.g. Transport versus Environment), or by interventions from Downing Street or the Treasury. Economic circumstances unavoidably have an impact on government's willingness to meet pressure-group demands. Against a background of continued pressure on public expenditure, demands for increases in service provision – or other changes in policy requiring more expenditure – are unlikely to be met. Even a Labour government with a willingness to increase public expenditure would face difficult choices, e.g. between funding nursery education and improving health care.

Delegating implementation to pressure groups

Although this is less common in Britain than in countries such as West Germany, government often shares its authority with pressure groups, delegating to them the responsibility for carrying out particular functions, or for providing particular services. Although this government reliance on private interest may seem to be a corporatist trait, its use tended to increase under the Thatcher Government as a result of the increasing reliance on 'contracting out' services which could not be completely abandoned. Examples include the provision of training funds through non-statutory training organisations (effectively employers' associations), which replaced the former statutory training boards in most sectors of the economy; the creation of self-regulatory organisations in the City of London with considerable disciplinary powers, including the ability to impose substantial fines; the involvement of the chambers of commerce in a number of government programmes; and the increased use of the voluntary sector for service delivery at the local level.

Some of the difficulties of voluntary organisations being used to implement policy are illustrated by the example of charities concerned with the Third World. Their position is further complicated by their charitable status which places limits on their political activities. Government financial support for their programmes through the Joint Funding Scheme is still only 10–15 per cent of the income of organisations such as Oxfam and Christian Aid, but after taking account of EU and other official grants, 'the proportion raised from voluntary contributions has been declining relative to official sources' (Robinson 1991, p. 166). The provision of government funds has the effect of emphasising the role of the voluntary organisations as effective providers of assistance where and when it is needed and 'plays down their political role in challenging the structural causes of poverty' (p. 176):

> Although it would be an exaggeration to claim that the government has deliberately sought to co-opt non-governmental organisations (NGOs) by offering them increased resources, it is nevertheless the case that voluntary agencies have become more muted in their criticism of the Overseas Development Administration . . . . NGOs have also been put on the defensive by critical remarks about their work by government Ministers.
>
> (Robinson 1991, p. 175)

Charity law is a special constraint for the aid lobbies, which have sometimes decided to set up separate campaigning organisations. More generally, it is more difficult to decide what the impact of these new responsibilities is on the traditional lobbying role of the pressure groups. They do enhance the attractiveness of group membership – for example, some employers' associations have advertised non-statutory training organisations as an additional selective benefit for their members. Administering the various functions does create new linkages with government. In the case of the Third World organisations, it has led to an improved dialogue with government and a less adversarial relationship. On the other hand, there is a risk of the groups being co-opted into government and losing their independence, while those groups that exercise delegated disciplinary powers may encounter resentment about the use of the powers among some of their members.

Conclusions

An attempt has been made in this chapter to generalise about the factors affecting pressure-group effectiveness. Although there are clearly some observable regularities in the ways in which successful groups operate, it must be emphasised that each pressure group faces a different situation, and has to develop and deploy a strategy to suit its particular circumstances.

Consider the example of the Society of Teachers Opposed to Physical Punishment (STOPP). Over twenty years after the group was formed in 1966, corporal punishment was banned in 1987 in state schools and for state-financed pupils in independent schools. The House of Commons accepted a House of Lords amendment abolishing corporal punishment on a free vote by 231 votes to 230 in 1986. STOPP thus attained its objective and was dissolved.

When STOPP was formed it faced an unpromising situation, including considerable hostility within schools. Its strategy was based first on ensuring that there could be no accusations of extremism, with its sponsors including a Conservative MP, a public-school headmaster and well-known peers. It kept to its single issue, refusing to become involved in wider educational controversies. It tried to change the language in which the debate about the issue was conducted. A founder member commented, 'Corporal punishment sounded like a respectable professional practice . . . . We talked about child beating.' Great care was taken over research to counteract claims that caning was in decline. 'It came to the point where we knew more about what was happening than anybody in the Department of Education' (The *Independent*, 24 November 1988).

Some London education authorities banned corporal punishment in the 1970s. In 1980 the Labour and Liberal party

conferences voted for abolition. In 1982 the NUT passed a resolution against corporal punishment in schools, followed in 1983 by
the head teachers' associations. Even more significant, in 1982 the
European Court found the UK guilty of breaching the European
Convention by not respecting parental objections to corporal
punishment. The Government then faced the prospect of paying
compensation, so it introduced a bill allowing parents to opt their
children out of corporal punishment. This bill was widely ridiculed
and was subsequently withdrawn, leading to the final successful
vote in 1986.

STOPP thus used a combination of methods. It was helped by
having one clear objective, but it also seems to have been very
careful in its choice of an appropriate strategy and tactics. It was
firm, informed and persuasive without being hysterical or fanatical.
Any group that wishes to be successful should bear these lessons in
mind.

The STOPP case is a straightforward one of a single-issue pressure group achieving its objective. More difficult to assess is the
case of the long-established pressure group with multiple objectives that is facing challenges to its traditional position, such as the
NFU. The farming press each week regularly carries letters from
readers and articles complaining about the embattled position of
farmers, the limited influence of the NFU, and the need to develop
new mechanisms to put across the farmers' case in an urban
society. These views receive some support from Smith (1991, p.
249):

> the power of the farmers has . . . started to decline. Farmers are now
> much less economically important and their decline in numbers
> suggests that any electoral influence they might have had has
> declined. New farm groups have developed, Conservative MPs have
> less attachment to rural issues than in the past and many on the right
> are critical of state support for agriculture. There has even been
> some cooling of relations between MAFF and the NFU.

It is true that farmers are facing increasing uncertainty as a
result of the moves towards the liberalisation of agricultural trade
as a result of the successful conclusion of the Uruguay Round
negotiations and the MacSharry reforms of the CAP. Some
smaller and marginal farmers are under increasing commercial
pressure because of such factors as changes in the forms of support
for hill farmers, and the likely impact of milk marketing reorgan-

isation on more remote farmers. However, under any set of policies, there are limits to the extent to which farmers could be shielded from the consequences of changes in technology and markets. It is the case that even large farmers do not always like being paid not to grow crops under 'set aside' or the amount of form-filling that is involved in obtaining CAP support. However, there must be checks on the payment of subsidies out of public funds, and farm incomes went up substantially in 1993.

It could therefore be argued that the NFU has coped well with a potentially difficult situation for its members. Smith acknowledges (1993, p. 112) that 'The NFU has followed a strategy of damage limitation by accepting the need for certain changes within agricultural policy without destroying the policy community nor the privileged position of the farmers.' 'Diversification' and conservation have provided new sources of grant income for farmers. The structure of MAFF remains dominated by the price and commodity groups which are oriented towards agricultural production. Admittedly, the implementation of some EU policies, such as that on nitrate sensitive areas which limits fertiliser use, will hit particular farmers hard (especially in some intensively farmed, largely arable areas) and contains no provision for compensation. Water pollution rules, which particularly affect dairy farmers, are more stringent and more strictly enforced. Scares that human health may be endangered by so-called 'mad cow disease' have not been handled very well.

Although the policy agenda of agriculture has changed from one that emphasises maximising production to one that gives a higher priority than before to protecting the environment, most farmers, particularly those operating on a large scale, remain a relatively privileged section of the community. They may not perceive that this is the case, but then farmers reacted with initial hostility to milk quotas which provided them with a new negotiable asset. Just how a relatively favourable outcome for farmers has been achieved remains a matter for argument: how much it is a consequence of government policy, and how much of NFU efforts, and how far the NFU has had to take account of other interests in the policy community to protect its position (Smith 1990b, 1993; Jordan, Maloney and McLaughlin, 1992d).

What the case of the NFU illustrates is that there is no clear methodology which can enable a clear assessment of group effectiveness. One has to look at policy outcomes – which in the case of agricultural policy have differential impacts on farmers – and then try to assess how far those policies have been influenced by the NFU as distinct from other actors. It is possible to fall back on perceptions of effectiveness, but if a group is perceived to be effective, this may itself be a cause of effectiveness rather than a way of measuring the dependent variable. If other key actors think that a group is effective, more heed may be taken of its views, creating a virtuous cycle for the group. I would place considerable emphasis on the way in which the NFU has been able to manage a changing and potentially threatening policy agenda. It may be, however, that a series of incremental changes in agricultural policy is adding up to a fundamental change in the policy context within which farmers operate. Some of the most important changes are coming from the EU and GATT levels, illustrating the limits of a purely domestic approach to assessing effectiveness.

The assessment of effectiveness thus remains a difficult task. It is probably easier to say which groups are ineffective, and to make general statements about apparent increases or declines in influence, than it is to estimate just how much influence a particular group has on policy outcomes. Even in relation to a single case study of a particular issue, the latter task is a difficult one, and one has to be very cautious about generalising from a particular example. Even so, if we are interested in finding out who wins and who loses in the political process, and *why* they win and lose, the question of effectiveness cannot be ignored by pressure-group analysts.

8

Conclusions: pressure groups and democracy

This concluding chapter will not attempt to summarise all the arguments reviewed in the book, but will concentrate on the implications of the discussion for the democratic process. In what ways do pressure groups contribute to, or detract from, democracy? The debate about democracy in Britain in the 1980s and 1990s has been overshadowed by the hegemony of the Conservative Party which has won four successive general elections. Britain started to acquire the characteristics of a dominant party system, notably increased factionalisation within the ruling party, which provided the most effective sources of opposition from within its own ranks. However, just as the dominant party systems in Italy and Japan ultimately crumbled, that of Britain is unlikely to be maintained for ever. Despite the sad and untimely loss of John Smith, the Labour Party seems to have its best chance since 1979 of becoming at least the largest party in the House of Commons to be elected in 1996 or 1997.

There has been a lively debate in Britain in the late 1980s and 1990s about the question of constitutional reform. The standard topics of discussion include: proportional representation; a bill of rights; reform of the House of Lords; legislative devolution for Scotland and Wales; and state funding of political parties. However, despite the decline in political party membership, and the rise of a whole generation of pressure groups, there has been little discussion of their future role in the political process. Even at a European level, much of the focus has been on political parties, with Article 138a of the Maastricht treaty stating:

> Political parties at European level are important as a factor for integration within the Union. They contribute to forming a European awareness and to expressing the political will of the citizens of the Union.

Yet pressure groups are also a means of expressing will, and potentially of forming a greater European awareness.

Part of the blame for the lack of any systematic discussion of pressure groups must rest with political scientists. The discussion of corporatism was an unavoidable one because it did try to provide a middle-level theoretical perspective for understanding rather widespread developments in relations between producer groups and governments which occurred particularly in the 1970s. Yet in the end, the debate became enervating, absorbed with disputes about definition, and expending time and energy fighting off intellectual raids from pluralists affronted at the invasion of their territory. Policy networks and policy communities became established as the new orthodoxy. What is remarkable about this debate is that there has been little discussion of the normative implications of having policy made in what are often relatively closed policy communities.

Perhaps this is not so surprising, however. At a time when politicians and political institutions are held in low esteem by the voting public (and not just in Britain), political scientists – other than those engaged in the constitutional reform debate – have been rather silent about the reinvigoration of democracy. Indeed, the constitutional reform debate does have a rather specific focus, and is inclined sometimes to place too much faith in the transformative potential of reforms such as the introduction of proportional representation.

The professionalisation of political science, although desirable in itself, does tend to encourage the discipline to be inward-looking. PhD students may be advised to locate their work within an established debate to maximise their chances of success, while senior academics always have to bear in mind the next research assessment exercise. All this discourages experimentation, risky work (which may not yield publications) and unorthodox views.

While stressing the importance of care with concepts, and the need for theoretically informed empirical work, the normative dimension should not be neglected. Political scientists should not aspire to be a secular priesthood, but they should show that they care about the health of democracy which, for all its failings, remains preferable to the alternatives.

The earlier chapters have sought to provide a comprehensive review and assessment of the British pressure-group literature. While still grounded in the literature, this chapter is more speculative, and is written more from the perspective of political scientist as citizen, rather than political scientist as professional observer.

The legacy of Thatcherism

It is relatively easy to trace a number of short-run impacts that Thatcherism has had on pressure-group activity, such as the downgrading of tripartite arrangements compared with the 1970s. Established producer interests such as the British Medical Association were also given a hard time. What is more difficult to assess are the long-run consequences of the Thatcher Government for pressure groups.

It is difficult to be certain about the ideological legacy of Thatcherism. Indeed, it is open to question whether Thatcherism was really an ideology, or simply a mixture of some strongly held convictions combined with an ability to be tactically flexible when putting the principles into practice. A parallel is often made with de Gaulle and Gaullism, not least because both Mrs Thatcher and de Gaulle were nationalists who sought to enhance their country's standing in the world. However, Gaullism disappeared as an ideology once de Gaulle left political life. His lasting legacy was the political institutions of the Fifth Republic, which have continued to serve France well.

Mrs Thatcher was unusual as a prime minister in that she had clear and strong views about the role of pressure groups in political life. She stated on *Weekend World* on 15 January 1984: 'I can give you a check-list now of the way in which we have tackled vested interest.' As a conviction politician, Mrs Thatcher had no time for the wishy-washy consensus, emerging from pressure-group discussions with government, which she saw as characteristic of much of the post-war period. Above all else, she detested corporatism which she saw as a form of socialism:

> Ted Heath's Government . . . proposed and implemented the most radical form of socialism ever contemplated by an elected British Government. It offered state control of prices and dividends, and the joint oversight of economic policy by a tripartite body representing the Trades Union Congress, the Confederation of British Industry and the Government, in return for trade union acquiescence in an incomes policy.
>
> (Thatcher 1993, p. 7)

One of the trends during the Thatcher period was an increased reliance on direct consultation with companies, which could be interpreted as a move towards a 'company state' (Grant 1993a). However, this trend could well have occurred without Mrs Thatcher as it was a reflection of such factors as globalisation and the key role of major companies in the international economy; the growing political sophistication of companies; and the weaknesses of trade associations. Indeed, Michael Heseltine, as noted in the last chapter, developed his own network of direct contacts with companies, although he also sought to revitalise trade associations, something which would not have happened under Mrs Thatcher.

Many commentators have drawn attention to the fact that there was nothing very liberal about Mrs Thatcher's approach to politics, even in the economic sense of the term. Ainley and Vickerstaff comment (1994, pp. 553–4):

> Our discussion suggests that in the transition from social democracy and its corporatist shell in Britain we have seen the development of an enterprise state which is neither genuinely liberal nor decentralised . . . . The return to a liberal free market model has been exaggerated as franchising represents a new form of state intervention in which public expenditure is no longer regulated through negotiation but via the individualised contract. The transition from corporatism therefore has not been towards only free market systems of allocation and accountability but also towards the franchise or state-induced enterprise model.

While Mrs Thatcher was in office, the traditional processes of consultation between middle-ranking civil servants and pressure groups continued very much as before. Long-established bureaucratic habits are not easily disturbed. Insofar as one can discern what John Major's attitude to pressure groups has been, it has been a return to 'business as usual', seeking to broker solutions on contentious issues such as Sunday trading. In the DTI, the sponsorship divisions have been restored, something that would not have happened under Mrs Thatcher. Groups such as the Institute of Directors have lost influence and members, and have met more resistance in their calls for deregulation and free-market policies.

What would really change the operations of pressure groups would be a fundamental change in the character of the civil service. The Next Steps programme has altered the way in which many important executive tasks are discharged within the civil service, but it has not had a profound effect on pressure-group activity. Plans to alter the character of the higher ranks of the civil service by contracting out much policy advice work would be a significant change. The European Commission relies substantially on contracted experts for information and advice. If the policy advice function were moved outside the civil service on a significant scale in Britain, pressure groups might find their role as trusted providers of information and expertise undermined. Establishing relations with the external providers of advice might be difficult.

Labour in office?

In 1994 the Conservative Government seemed to be suffering from a worse dose than usual of the 'midterm blues'. To the outside observer, the Government gave the impression of running out of ideas and of talent. Just as the Labour Party had sacrificed its strongest electoral card in the 'winter of discontent' of 1978–9 – the claim that it was the only party that could deal with the unions – the Conservatives seemed to have surrendered their strongest vote-winning card, the claim that they would hold down taxes. The long-run increase in crime made them vulnerable on one of their other strongest issues – law and order – whereas Tony Blair had constructed an effective policy response for Labour with the slogan 'tough on crime and tough on the causes of crime'. There was also a concern about the fabric of society in terms of such issues as unemployment, the health service, education and the homeless. Tony Blair's Christian Socialism offered a vision to tackle these problems, in the way that Harold Wilson had offered a vision of 'scientific socialism' before Labour's admittedly narrow victory in 1964. I make no claim to be an elections expert, but as a non-partisan observer, it did seem to me at the time of writing (1994) that there might have been one of those sea changes in the mood of the British people that had led to a Labour victory in 1964 and to Mrs Thatcher's victory in 1979.

It is not the purpose of this book to offer electoral predictions, however, and one should never underestimate the ability of the Conservative Party to recover from a difficult situation. Very little is certain in politics – which is what makes its study so interesting. Nevertheless, it is worth briefly considering the consequences of a Labour victory in 1996 or 1997. Much would, of course, depend on the nature of the victory. A majority of, say, thirty seats over all other parties would create a very different situation from one in which Labour was the largest party, but had to rely on support from minority parties to get its legislation through Parliament. In that situation, pressure groups would start to give greater attention to Westminster.

A Labour victory would create considerable initial uncertainty. Many of the readers of this book will not be able to remember a Labour government in office, and would find Harold Wilson's claim that Labour was the natural party of government a strange one (but Wilson did win four of the five general elections he fought). Very few ministers would have held ministerial office before. Quite senior civil servants would have spent their entire careers working under a Conservative government where being involved in, for example, a major privatisation was a shrewd career move. That is not to say that civil servants would fail to try and serve the new government with their customary loyalty and efficiency – indeed many of them might privately welcome a change:

> There has been a loss of mutual confidence and respect between Conservative ministers and many officials. This has gone so far that it is difficult to see how an effective working relationship can be rebuilt without a change of government. A new, non-Conservative government ought very early on to decide and to make explicit its policy towards the civil service which it inherits.
>
> (Plowden 1994, p. 139)

For pressure groups, there would also be considerable uncertainty. Sophisticated groups like the CBI and NFU have, of course, carefully followed the development of Labour policy and kept in touch with the relevant shadow spokespersons. One would expect the trade unions, who have gone through a significant programme of modernisation and merger, to move back to the centre of the stage. The pursuit of a full-employment commitment might lead to a drift back towards tripartism, particularly if an incomes policy were adopted, which some analysts think is not entirely off the agenda (Kessler 1994). A Labour government would then come up against the limitations of a corporatist strategy in a state like Britain with a liberal tradition.

Perhaps the greatest uncertainty is how Labour policy towards the European Union would develop, although that in turn would also depend on the political composition and outlook of other major European governments. Although they have been submerged in the interests of party unity, there are almost as many fault lines in the Labour Party as in the Conservative Party over Europe. Just how Britain's relationships with the EU developed under a Labour government would have an important influence on the political context in which pressure groups operate.

The case for pressure groups reviewed

Des Wilson, well known as a campaigner, has provided a list of key justifications for the existence of community/cause pressure groups. Of course, the population of pressure groups is also made up of sectional groups. Wilson has no time for 'vested interests, whose cause is usually maintenance of the status quo irrespective of the implications for the community' (Wilson 1984, p. 2). Such groups are seen by him as part of a pattern of failure 'by our institutions, failures rooted in a deep bias towards the status quo, and vested interest in power and wealth'. It is in these and other failures 'that we find the outstanding argument for pressure groups' (p. 20). I am less sympathetic to the notion of 'cause groups good, sectional groups bad' which underpins much argument about pressure groups and the democratic process – a stance which ultimately reduces to a slightly more sophisticated way of saying one likes those pressure groups whose values one shares. Idealists, and those seeking to promote change, like Wilson, have a right to organise and be heard, but so do realists seeking to defend existing arrangements.

Wilson outlines seven key justifications for the existence of pressure groups, and the first three of these provide a good basis for reviewing many of the arguments about the contribution of pressure groups to democracy. The last four are less convincing and will be considered more briefly. The first is the argument that 'There is more to democracy than the occasional vote' (p. 21). Wilson is an enthusiast for participatory democracy, and he regards pressure groups as one way in which participation could take place. The counter-argument for representative democracy is that many people consider that there are more meaningful or enjoyable activities in life than politics, and are therefore prepared to have persons sharing their general political outlook acting on their behalf.

Wilson deals with the argument that opposition parties provide a means whereby people can exercise their democratic rights by maintaining that they 'are themselves part of the governing system . . . . Often specialist pressure groups are more effective than all-issue political parties in opposing "the system" (p. 21). What is clear is that the membership of cause groups has increased as the membership of political parties has declined. Many people are active in both political parties and cause groups, but it would seem that political parties have often seemed too unwelcoming, bureaucratic and preoccupied with questions of dogma to younger activists with a desire to bring about changes in society.

Wilson claims that pressure groups counterbalance two inherent weaknesses in democracy, the first being that democracy 'does *not* work for all people' and that 'Pressure groups offer a chance for minorities and disadvantaged groups to argue their case' (p. 22). This goes to the heart of the problem about democracy, which is that it is a majoritarian form of government which nevertheless aspires, in its defensible forms, to protect minority rights. The second inherent weakness identified by Wilson is that electioneering encourages a short-term perspective on issues.

The first weakness identified by Wilson raises such fundamental issues about the relationship between pressure groups and democracy that some space will have to be devoted to considering these problems before returning to Wilson's other arguments. The principal counter-argument is that pressure-group activity tends to reinforce existing biases within the political system rather than counteracting them. The idea that it is more difficult to organise general than particular interests recalls the discussion of Olson's theory of pressure groups in Chapter 2. What is evident from the discussion in the book as a whole is that business interests have tended to strengthen their privileged position in the 1980s and 1990s, especially at the EU level. There are a number of reasons for this trend: the existence of a government in Britain over this period which, even if it was not well disposed to particular business-interest associations, sought to promote business interests; the weakening of the principal countervailing force – organised labour – with environmental groups hardly an adequate substitute; and the growing sophistication of the political operations of firms. All governments want a successful economy, and this means that there has to be a dialogue with business, whose views must be seriously considered. However, it may be that the balance has swung too far in the direction of business interests, and that the construction of the political agenda pays too much attention to what would serve the market economy, and not enough to the needs of less-advantaged members of the population.

Another problem arises from what the Aberdeen group's data show to be the overwhelmingly middle-class, highly educated composition of the memberships of the cause groups they studied. It must be emphasised that not all highly educated members of the middle class join pressure groups: one is talking about a subset of a subset of the population. The evidence seems to suggest that those who join one group are likely to join others as well. This group of highly educated 'joiners' may have values that diverge quite substantially from those of the population at large, and yet be able to influence the political decision-making process in a significant way through their campaigning activities so that popular opinion and government decisions increasingly diverge. That in turn could lead to a further decline in confidence in the institutions of government.

That is to put the position at its most pessimistic. It is important to distinguish between the social composition of a pressure group and the objectives for which it is fighting. This is a point that has been made particularly by supporters of the environmental movement. Porritt and Winner argue that Greens are concentrated in the 'caring' professions, and are usually committed to a non-materialist lifestyle. Such individuals do not fit in 'too neatly with the role assigned to them in the Marxist demonology as oppressors of the working class' (1988, pp. 182–3). That may be so, but what about those members of the population who do not have a university education and want to pursue a materialist lifestyle? There is a danger of university-educated activists assuming that their values ought to be shared by everyone else. It also has to be recognised that some amenity society activity is essentially concerned with protecting property values and preserving the exclusive social identity of particular locations.

Perhaps an even stronger counter-argument is that the increased political activity of environmental groups has not led to major changes in policy outcomes (some activists would claim that more can be achieved by 'green consumerism') and that the underlying bias favours business interests:

> The environment lobby now has greater resources and a much higher profile than it had in the late 1970s. But it has a limited and erratic impact at the national level. Its influence has been great in spheres of policy like the countryside . . . . But there are other areas in which business interests still predominate. On roads there may be isolated victories like withdrawal of the Oxleas Wood and Hereford by-pass schemes. But the basic policy continues.
>
> (Young 1993, p. 23)

Having digressed to consider the fundamental issues raised by Wilson's first point, it is now possible to return to his other arguments. As noted earlier, Wilson argues that a second inherent weakness in parliamentary democracy is that the need to win elections leads to short-term political considerations prevailing over the longer-term interests of the country. I am less confident than he is that cause groups are able to take a long-term perspective. Too often they are ensnared in the assumptions of long-established policies, arguing for more resources to be devoted to such policies, or for improvements to be made in them, rather than for fundamental changes designed to meet long-term problems.

Wilson's third main argument is that 'Pressure groups improve surveillance of government' (Wilson 1984, p. 23). Pressure groups can help to expose information which would otherwise remain secret. There have been important instances where pressure groups such as the Child Poverty Action Group have influenced public policy by leaking Cabinet documents. However, occasional exposures of this kind have to be set against a system of government which is still permeated by a preoccupation with secrecy. Because the desirability of greater freedom of information has become a position shared by many academics and journalists commenting on British government, it is worth noting that there is a counter-view which argues that open government would bring costs as well as benefits, particularly in relation to pressure-group activity. Douglas Hurd has commented that, if freedom of information 'simply means freedom for pressure groups to extract from the system only those pieces of information which buttress their own cause, then conceivably the result might be greater confusion and worse government' (Royal Institute of Public Administration Report, 1986, p. 1).

Wilson's other argument in favour of pressure groups as a means of improving surveillance of government is a more conventional one. He points out that they can bring to the attention of ministers and civil servants options and information of which they would not otherwise be aware. This is an aspect of pressure-group activity that is generally valued by government.

Wilson's other four arguments are less impressive. The argument that 'Pressure groups combat other pressure groups' (1984, p. 24), although particularly directed at redressing the influence of sectional groups, is really a reflection of conventional pluralist wisdom about countervailing groups. The argument that pressure groups persist in fighting for causes in which the media take only a short-term interest is a valid one, particularly in relation to the example Wilson gives of lead in petrol, but it is not a central argument in favour of pressure-group activity *per se*. The argument that 'Community/cause groups offer people the weapons to fight on their own behalf' (p. 25) reflects Wilson's belief in the value of political participation, and the way in which group activity can build up the skills required for effective collective action. His final argument, that 'Pressure groups relieve frustration' (p. 25) is a double-edged one. No doubt they can act as a safety-valve, and give people a sense of hope, but in doing so they may be serving more to promote political and social stability than to bring about real change.

Although I do not agree with a number of his arguments, I agree with Wilson's general conclusion that 'pressure groups are not a threat to a genuine democracy, but a real contributor' (p. 25). I would insist that sectional groups have a contribution to make as well as cause groups. If the stake which 'vested interests' have is simply brushed aside, then serious damage may, quite unintentionally, be inflicted on the economy or on professions which make a worthwhile contribution to the community.

The limits to pressure-group power

If pressure groups were allowed to accumulate too much influence, then there would be a risk for democracy. As it is, pressure groups operate in a political system in which they are checked by other political forces. First, as has been pointed out a number of times, public opinion strongly influences the context in which pressure groups operate. Environmental policy has been given a high priority in part because of accumulating scientific evidence about the seriousness of environmental problems, but also because the public has become more concerned about environmental questions, and politicians of all parties have felt the need to make some response to this shifting climate of opinion. From the perspective of many environmentalists, the changes in public policy have been inadequate, but then environmental concerns have to be balanced against other considerations, particularly economic ones.

Pressure groups are also held in check by political parties, and by government ministers anxious to address a wider political audience than that of a sectional interest or cause group. Broadly based political parties have to appeal beyond the relatively narrow concerns of most pressure groups to win elections. Ministers wish to build their political and legislative reputations. Occasionally, an MP may build his or her reputation through the successful passage of a private member's bill, but in general it is ministers who take important legislative initiatives.

Pressure-group power is limited: it is based on the ability to persuade and to influence, rather than to take decisions or, with certain exceptions, to veto them. Groups which have enjoyed significant power at particular periods of time, such as the trade unions, have usually experienced a public reaction against them. Nevertheless, one should not be too complacent about the position of pressure groups in the political system. The cards are often stacked in favour of established insider groups. Policy communities are often too narrowly based, or too closed to new influences, producing policy solutions that represent incremental adjustments to existing policies.

Pressure groups do make a significant contribution to democracy, one which can be understood if we visualise a situation in which pressure groups were either banned or disregarded. Not only is the freedom to associate an important democratic principle, but pressure groups also offer an important mechanism through which the ruled can influence the rulers between elections. They also contribute to the quality of policy-making by bringing the practical experience of, for example, business persons, doctors, teachers or clients of the social services into what might otherwise be a rather insular debate in Whitehall about the development of policy. *Government* policy can only serve as *public* policy if it is based on consultations with interested publics.

References

Ainley, P. and Vickerstaff, S. (1994), 'Transitions from corporatism: the privatisation of policy failure', *Contemporary Record*, **7** (3), pp. 541–56.

Amery, L.S. (1947), *Thoughts on the Constitution*, Oxford: Oxford University Press.

Arp, H.A. (1993), 'Technical regulation and politics: the interplay between economic interests and environmental policy goals in EC car emission legislation', in *European Integration and Environmental Policy*, Liefferink, J.D., Lowe, P.D. and Nol, A.P.J. (eds.), London: Belhaven.

Atkinson, M.M. and Coleman, W.D. (1985), 'Corporatism and industrial policy', in *Organized Interests and the State*, Cawson, A. (ed.), London: Sage.

Baldwin, N. (1990), 'The House of Lords', in *Parliament and Pressure Politics*, Rush, M. (ed.), Oxford: Clarendon Press.

Barr, G. (1992), 'The anti-poll tax movement: an insider's view of an outsider group', *Talking Politics*, **4** (3), pp. 143–7.

Beer, S. (1956), 'Pressure groups and parties in Britain', *American Political Science Review*, **50** (1), pp. 1–23.

Beer, S. (1965), *Modern British Politics*, London: Faber and Faber.

Beer, S. (1982), *Britain Against Itself*, London: Faber and Faber.

Berry, S. (1992), 'Lobbyists: techniques of the political "insiders"', *Government and Opposition*, 45, pp. 220–32.

Bose, A. (1991), 'Aid and the business lobby', in *Britain's Overseas Aid Since 1979*, Bose, A. and Burnell, P. (eds.), Manchester: Manchester University Press.

Bown, F. (1990), 'The defeat of the Shops Bill, 1986', in *Parliament and Pressure Politics*, Rush, M. (ed.), Oxford: Clarendon Press.

Boyle, E. (1971), Contribution to E. Boyle and A. Crosland in conversation with M. Kogan, *The Politics of Education*, Harmondsworth: Penguin.

Brickman, R., Jasanoff, S. and Ilgen, T. (1985), *Controlling Chemicals: The politics of regulation in Europe and the United States*, Ithaca: Cornell University Press.

Brittan, S. (1964), *Steering the Economy*, Harmondsworth: Penguin.

Brittan, S. (1975), 'The economic contradictions of democracy', *British Journal of Political Science*, 5, pp. 129–59.

Brittan, S. (1987a), ' "The economic contradictions of democracy" revisited', *Political Quarterly*, **60** (2), pp. 190–203.

Brittan, S. (1987b), *The Role and Limits of Government*, Aldershot: Wildwood House.

Brittan, S. (1989), 'The Thatcher Government's economic policy', Esmee Fairbairn Lecture, University of Lancaster Economics Department.

Brooke, R. (1989), *Managing the Enabling Authority*, Harrow: Longman.

Browne, W.P. (1990), 'Organized interests and their interest niches: a search for pluralism in a policy domain', *Journal of Politics*, **52** (2), pp. 477–509.

Bruce-Gardyne, J. (1986), *Ministers and Mandarins*, London: Sidgwick and Jackson.

Buksti, J.A. and Johansen, L.N. (1979), 'Variations in organizational participation in government: the case of Denmark', *Scandinavian Political Studies*, **2** (new series) (3), pp. 197–220.

Burson-Marsteller (1991), *Lobbying the EC. The views of the policymakers*, Brussels: Burson-Marsteller.

Cawson, A. (1992), 'Interests, groups and public policy-making: the case of the European consumer electronics industry', in *Organized Interests and the European Community*, Greenwood, J., Grote, J.R. and Ronit, K. (eds.), London: Sage.

Christiansen, L. and Dowding, K. (1994), 'Pluralism or state autonomy? The case of Amnesty International (British Section): the insider/outsider group', *Political Studies*, **42** (1), pp. 15–24.

Churchill, W. (1930), 'Parliamentary government and the economic problem', Romanes Lecture, Oxford.

Coates, David (1972), *Teachers Unions and Interest Group Politics*, London: Cambridge University Press.

Coates, Dudley (1984), 'Food law: Brussels, Whitehall and town hall', in *Policies into Practice*, Lewis, D. and Wallace, H. (eds.), London: Heinemann.

Coffin, C. (1987), *Working with Whitehall*, London: Confederation of British Industry.

Cox, G., Lowe, P. and Winter, M. (1986), 'The state and the farmer: perspectives on agricultural policy', in *Agriculture: People and Policies*, Cox, G., Lowe, P. and Winter, M. (eds.), London: Allen and Unwin.

Danton de Rouffignac, P. (1991), *Presenting Your Case to Europe*, London: Mercury.

Davies, M. (1985), *Politics of Pressure*, London: BBC Publications.

Devlin Commission (1972), *Report of the Commission of Inquiry into Industrial and Commercial Representation*, London: Association of British Chambers of Commerce/Confederation of British Industry.

Doig, A. (1986), 'Access to Parliament and the rise of the professional lobbyist', *Public Money*, **5** (4), pp. 39–43.

Dowding, K. (1994a), 'Rational mobilisation', in *Contemporary Political Studies, Volume Two*, Dunleavy, P. and Stanyer, J. (eds.), Belfast: Political Studies Association.

Dowding, K. (1994b), 'Policy networks: don't stretch a good idea too far', in *Contemporary Political Studies, Volume One*, Dunleavy, P. and Stanyer, J. (eds.), Belfast: Political Studies Association.

Dowse, R.E. and Hughes, J. (1977), 'Sporadic interventionists', *Political Studies*, **25** (1), pp. 84–92.

Dudley, G. (1983), 'The road lobby: a declining force', in *Pressure Politics*, Marsh, D. (ed.), London: Junction Books.

Dunleavy, P. (1988), 'Group identities and individual influence: reconstructing the theory of interest groups', *British Journal of Political Science*, **18** (1), pp. 21–49.

Dunleavy, P. (1991), *Democracy, Bureaucracy and Public Choice*, Hemel Hempstead: Harvester Wheatsheaf.

Eberlie, R. (1993), 'The Confederation of British Industry and policy-making in the European Community', in *Lobbying in the European Community*, Mazey, S. and Richardson, J. (eds.), Oxford: Oxford University Press.

Eckstein, H. (1960), *Pressure Group Politics: The case of the British Medical Association*, London: Allen and Unwin.

Edwards, R. (1988), 'Spirit of outrage', *New Statesman and Society*, 29 July, pp. 16 and 18.

Elbaum, B. and Lazonick, W. (eds.) (1986), *The Decline of the British Economy*, Oxford: Clarendon Press.

Elliott, B., Bechhofer, F., McCrone, D. and Black, S. (1982), 'Bourgeois social movements in Britain: repertoires and responses', *Sociological Review*, **30** (1), pp. 71–94.

Field, F. (1982) *Poverty and Politics*, London: Heinemann.

Finer, S.E. (1958), *Anonymous Empire*, London: Pall Mall.

Franklin, M. (1994), 'Food policy formation in the UK/EC', in *The Politics of Food*, Henson, S. and Gregory, S. (eds.), Reading: Department of Agricultural Economics and Management, University of Reading.

Gardner, J.N. (1991), *Effective Lobbying in the European Community*, Deventer: Kluwer.

Garner, R. (1993), *Animals, Politics and Morality*, Manchester: Manchester University Press.

Gilmour, I. (1978), *Inside Right*, London: Quartet.

Gilmour, I. (1983), *Britain Can Work*, Oxford: Martin Robertson.

Grant, W. (1978), 'Insider groups, outsider groups and interest group strategies in Britain', University of Warwick Department of Politics Working Paper No. 19.

Grant, W. (1983), 'Chambers of Commerce in the UK system of business interest representation', University of Warwick Department of Politics Working Paper No. 32.

Grant, W. (1993a), *Business and Politics in Britain*, 2nd edn, London: Macmillan.

Grant, W. (1993b), *The Politics of Economic Policy*, Hemel Hempstead: Harvester Wheatsheaf.

Grant, W. (forthcoming), *Autos, Smog and Pollution Control*, Cheltenham: Edward Elgar.

Grant, W. and Marsh, D. (1977), *The CBI*, London: Hodder and Stoughton.

Grant, W. and Streeck, W. (1985), 'Large firms and the representation of business interests in the UK and West German construction industry' in *Organized Interests and the State: Studies in meso-corporatism*, Cawson, A. (ed.), London: Sage.

Grant, W., Nekkers, J. and van Waarden, F. (eds.) (1991), *Organizing Business for War*, Oxford: Berg.

Grant, W., Paterson, W.E. and Whitston, C. (1988), *Government and the Chemical Industry*, Oxford: Clarendon Press.

Grantham, C. and Seymour-Ure, C. (eds.) (1990), 'Political consultants', in *Parliament and Pressure Politics*, Rush, M. (ed.), Oxford: Clarendon Press.

Green, M.L. (1993), 'The politics of big business in the Single Market Program', paper presented for the European Community Studies Association conference, Washington DC.

Greenwood, J. and Jordan, G. (1993), 'The United Kingdom: a changing kaleidoscope', in *National Public and Private EC Lobbying*, Van Schendelen, M.P.C.M. (ed.), Aldershot: Dartmouth.

Greenwood, J. and Ronit, K. (1992), 'Established and emergent sectors: organized interests at the European level in the pharmaceutical industries and the new biotechnologies', in *Organized Interests and the European Community*, Greenwood, J., Grote, J.R. and Ronit, K. (eds.) London: Sage.

Greenwood, J., Grote, J.R. and Ronit, K. (1992), 'Introduction: organized interests and the transnational dimension', in *Organized Interests and the European Community*, Greenwood, J., Grote, J.R. and Ronit, K. (eds.), London: Sage.

Hall, P. (1986), *Governing the Economy*, Cambridge: Polity Press.

Harvey, B. (1993), 'Lobbying in Europe: the experience of voluntary organisations', in *Lobbying in the European Community*, Mazey, S. and Richardson, J. (eds.), Oxford: Oxford University Press.

Heclo, H. and Wildavsky, A. (1974), *The Private Government of Public Money*, London: Macmillan.

Hindell, K. and Simms, M. (1974), 'How the abortion lobby worked', in *Pressure Groups in Britain*, Kimber, R. and Richardson, J.J. (eds.), London: Dent.

Holbeche, B. (1986), 'Policy and influence: MAFF and the NFU', *Public Policy and Administration*, 1, pp. 40–7.

House of Commons (1985), *First Report from the Select Committee on Members' Interests, 1984/85*, London: HMSO.

Hull, R. (1993), 'Lobbying Brussels: a view from within', in *Lobbying in the European Community*, Mazey, S. and Richardson, J. (eds.), Oxford: Oxford University Press.

Isaac-Henry, K. (1984), 'Taking stock of the local authority associations', *Public Administration*, **62** (2), pp. 129–46.

Jordan, A.G. and Richardson, J. (1987), *Government and Pressure Groups in Britain*, Oxford: Clarendon Press.

Jordan, G. (1990), 'The pluralism of pluralism: an anti-theory?', *Political Studies*, **38** (2), pp. 286–301.

Jordan, G. (1994), 'Why bumble bees fly: accounting for public interest participation', paper presented at ECPR Joint Sessions, Madrid.

Jordan, G., Maloney, W. and McLaughlin, A. (1992a), 'What is studied when pressure groups are studied?: policy participants and pressure groups', British Interest Group Project Working Paper No. 1, University of Aberdeen.

Jordan, G., Maloney, W. and McLaughlin, A. (1992b), 'Insiders, outsiders and political access', British Interest Group Project Working Paper No. 3, University of Aberdeen.

Jordan, G., Maloney, W. and McLaughlin, A. (1992c), 'Assumptions about the role of groups in the policy process: the British policy community approach', British Interest Group Project Working Paper No. 4, University of Aberdeen.

Jordan, G., Maloney, W. and McLaughlin, A. (1992d), 'Policy-making in agriculture: "primary" policy community or specialist policy communities', British Interest Group Project Working Paper No. 5, University of Aberdeen.

Jordan, G., Maloney, W. and McLaughlin, A. (1994a), 'Collective action and the public interest problem: drawing a line under Olson', in *Contemporary Political Studies, Volume Two*, Dunleavy, P. and Stanyer, J. (eds.), Belfast: Political Studies Association.

Jordan, G., Maloney, W. and McLaughlin, A. (1994b), 'Interest groups: a marketing perspective on membership', in *Contemporary Political Studies, Volume Two*, Dunleavy, P. and Stanyer, J. (eds.), Belfast: Political Studies Association.

Judge, D. (1990a), 'Parliament and interest representation', in *Parliament and Pressure Politics*, Rush, M. (ed.), Oxford: Clarendon Press.

Judge, D. (1990b), *Parliament and Industry*, Aldershot: Dartmouth.

Judge, D. (1993), *The Parliamentary State,* London: Sage.

Kessler, S. (1994), 'Incomes policy', *British Journal of Industrial Relations*, **32** (2), pp. 181–99.

King, R. (1985), 'Corporatism and the Local Economy' in *The Political Economy of Corporatism*, Grant, W. (ed.), London: Macmillan.

Kingdon, J.W. (1984), *Agendas, Alternatives and Public Policies*, New York: Harper-Collins.

Kohler-Koch, B. (1993), 'Germany: fragmented but strong lobbying', in *National Public and Private EC Lobbying,* Van Schendelen, M.P.C.M. (ed.), Aldershot: Dartmouth.

Kohler-Koch, B. (1994), 'Changing patterns of interest intermediation in the European Union', *Government and Opposition*, **29** (2), pp. 166–80.

Lawson, N. (1992), *The View From No. 11: Memoirs of a Tory Radical*, London: Bantam.

Lazonick, W. (1986), 'The Cotton Industry', in *The Decline of the British Economy*, Elbaum, B. and Lazonick, W. (eds.), Oxford: Clarendon Press.

Lindblom, C.E. (1977), *Politics and Markets*, New York: Basic Books.

Lively, J. (1975), *Democracy*, Oxford: Basil Blackwell.

Lowe, P. and Goyder, J. (1983), *Environmental Groups in Politics*, London: Allen and Unwin.

Lynn, L.H. and McKeown, T.J. (1988), *Organizing Business: Trade Associations in America and Japan*, Washington, DC: American Enterprise Institute.

MacDougall, D. (1987), *Don and Mandarin: Memoirs of an Economist*, London: John Murray.

McLaughlin, A. and Jordan, G. (1993) 'The rationality of lobbying in Europe: why are Euro-groups so numerous and so weak? Some evidence from the car industry', in *Lobbying in the European Community*, Mazey, S. and Richardson, J. (eds.), Oxford: Oxford University Press.

McLaughlin, A., Jordan, G. and Maloney, W.A. (1993), 'Corporate lobbying in the European Community', *Journal of Common Market Studies*, **31** (2), pp. 191–212.

McLeay, E.M. (1990), 'Defining policing policies and the political agenda', *Political Studies*, **38** (4), pp. 620–37.

Maddox, B. (1994), 'Lobby groups left to carry Green banner', *Financial Times*, 5–6 March 1994, p. 8.

MAFF (1987), *Survey of Consumer Attitudes to Food Additives*, London: HMSO.

Malhan, N. (1994), 'European integration and German federalism: the immigration issue', paper presented at the Political Studies Association conference, Swansea.

Marsh, D. and Chambers, J. (1981), *Abortion Politics*, London: Junction Books.

Marsh, D. and Read, M. (1988), *Private Members Bills*, London: Cambridge University Press.

Martinelli, A. and Grant, W. (1991), 'Conclusion', in *International Markets and Global Firms*, Martinelli, A. (ed.), London: Sage.

May, T. and Nugent, N. (1982), 'Insiders, outsiders and thresholders: corporatism and pressure group strategies in Britain', paper presented at Political Studies Association conference, University of Kent.

Mazey, S. and Mitchell, J. (1993), 'Europe of the regions? Territorial interests and European integration: the Scottish experience', in *Lobbying in the European Community*, Mazey, S. and Richardson, J. (eds.), Oxford: Oxford University Press.

Mazey, S. and Richardson, J. (1992a), 'British pressure groups in the European Community', *Parliamentary Affairs*, **45** (1), pp. 92–127.

Mazey, S. and Richardson, J. (1992b), 'Environmental groups and the EC: challenges and opportunities', *Environmental Politics*, **4** (1), pp. 109–28.

Mazey, S. and Richardson, J. (1993a), 'Introduction', in *Lobbying in the European Community*, Mazey, S. and Richardson J. (eds.), Oxford: Oxford University Press.

Mazey, S. and Richardson, J. (1993b), 'Conclusion: a European policy style?', in *Lobbying in the European Community*, Mazey, S. and Richardson, J. (eds.), Oxford: Oxford University Press.

Mazey, S. and Richardson, J. (1993c), 'EC policy making: an emerging policy style?', in *European Integration and Environmental Policy*, Liefferink, J.D., Lowe, P.D. and Mol A.P.J. (eds.), London: Belhaven.

Mazey, S. and Richardson, J. (1993d), 'Effective business lobbying in Brussels', *European Business Journal*, **5** (4), pp. 14–24.

Medhurst, K. (1991), 'Reflections on the Church of England and Politics at a Moment of Transition', *Parliamentary Affairs*, 44 (2), pp. 240–61.

Medhurst, K. and Moyser, G. (1988), *Church and Politics in a Secular Age*, Oxford: Clarendon Press.

Miller, C. (1990), *Lobbying*, Oxford: Basil Blackwell.

Miller, D. and Reilly, J. (1994), 'Food and the media: the reporting of food "risks"', in *The Politics of Food*, Henson, S. and Gregory, S. (eds.), Reading: Department of Agricultural Economics and Management, University of Reading.

Mills, M. (1992), *The Politics of Dietary Change*, Aldershot: Dartmouth.

Mitchell, N.J. (1987), 'Changing pressure-group politics: the case of the Trades Union Congress, 1976/84', *British Journal of Political Science*, 17, pp. 509–17.

Moe, T.M. (1980), *The Organisation of Interests*, Chicago: Chicago University Press.

Moran, M. (1983), 'Power, policy and the City of London', *Capital and Politics*, King, R. (ed.), London: Routledge and Kegan Paul.

Moravcsik, A. (1991), 'Negotiating the Single European Act: national interests and conventional statecraft in the European Community', *International Organization*, 45, pp. 19–56.

Nettl, J.P. (1965), 'Consensus or elite domination: the case of business', *Political Studies*, 8, pp. 22–44.

Newby, H., Bell, C., Rose, D. and Saunders, P. (1978), *Property, Paternalism and Power: Class and control in rural England*, London: Hutchinson.

Newton, K. (1976), *Second City Politics*, Oxford: Oxford University Press.

Norton, P. (1990), 'Public legislation', in *Parliament and Pressure Politics*, Rush, M. (ed.), Oxford: Clarendon Press.

Offe, C. and Wiesenthal, H. (1985), 'Two logics of collective action', in *Disorganised Capitalism*, Offe, C. (principal author), Cambridge: Cambridge University Press.

Olson, M. (1965), *The Logic of Collective Action*, Cambridge, Mass.: Harvard University Press.

Olson, M. (1982), *The Rise and Decline of Nations*, New Haven: Yale University Press.

Plowden, W. (1985), 'The culture of Whitehall', in *Understanding the Civil Service*, Englefield, D. (ed.), Harlow: Longman.

Plowden, W. (1994), *Ministers and Mandarins*, London: Institute for Public Policy Research.

Porritt, J. and Winner, D. (1988), *The Coming of the Greens*, London: Fontana.

Pratt, H.J. (1993), *Gray Agendas: Interest groups and public pensions in Canada, Britain, and the United States*, Ann Arbor: University of Michigan Press.

Presthus, R. (1964), *Men at the Top*, New York: Oxford University Press.

Presthus, R. (1973), *Elite Accommodation in Canadian Politics*, London: Cambridge University Press.

Presthus, R. (1974), *Elites in the Policy Process*, London: Cambridge University Press.

Public Policy Consultants (1987), 'The Government Report', London: Public Policy Consultants.

Rhodes, R.A.W. and Marsh, D. (1992), 'Policy networks in British politics: a critique of existing approaches', in *Policy Networks in British Government*, Marsh, D. and Rhodes, R.A.W. (eds.), Oxford: Clarendon Press.

Rhodes, R.A.W., Hardy, B. and Pudney, K. (1981), 'Public interest groups in central/local relations in England and Wales', *Public Administration Bulletin*, no. 36, pp. 17–36.

Richardson, J. (1993), 'Interest group behaviour in Britain: continuity and change', in *Pressure Groups*, Richardson, J. (ed.), Oxford: Oxford University Press.

Richardson, J. and Jordan, G. (1979), *Governing Under Pressure*, Oxford: Martin Robertson.

Richardson, J., Maloney, W. and Rüdig, W. (1992), 'The dynamics of policy change: lobbying and water privatization', *Public Administration*, **70** (2), pp. 157–75.

Robinson, M. (1991), 'An uncertain partnership: the Overseas Development Administration and the voluntary sector in the 1980s', in *Britain's Overseas Aid Since 1979*, Bose, A. and Burnell, P. (eds.), Manchester: Manchester University Press.

Robinson, M. (1992), *The Greening of British Party Politics*, Manchester: Manchester University Press.

Rose, R. (1974), *Politics in England Today*, London: Faber and Faber.

Rucht, D. (1993), '"Think globally, act locally?" Needs, forms and problems of cross-national cooperation among environmental groups', in *European Integration and Environmental Policy*, Liefferink, J.D., Lowe, P. and Mol, A.P.J. (eds.), London: Belhaven.

Rush, M. (1990), 'Select Committees' in *Parliament and Pressure Politics*, Rush, M. (ed.), Oxford: Clarendon Press.

Salisbury, R.H. (1984), 'Interest representation: the dominance of institutions', *American Political Science Review*, 78, pp. 64–76.

Sandholtz, W. and Zysman, J. (1989), 'Recasting the European bargain', *World Politics*, **42** (4), pp. 95–128.

Sargent, J.A. (1993), 'The corporate benefits of lobbying: the British case and its relevance to the European Community', in *Lobbying in the European Community*, Mazey, S. and Richardson, J. (eds.), Oxford: Oxford University Press.

Schattschneider, E.E. (1960), *The Semisovereign People*, New York: Holt, Rinehart and Winston.

Schmitter, P.C. and Streeck, W. (1981), 'The organisation of business interests: a research design to study the associative action of business in the advanced industrial societies of Western Europe', International Institute of Management labour market policy discussion paper.

Self, P. and Storing, H.J. (1962), *The State and the Farmer*, London: Allen and Unwin.

Seyd, P. and Whiteley, P. (1992), *Labour's Grass Roots: The politics of party membership*, Oxford: Clarendon Press.

Smith, M.J. (1988), 'Consumers and British agricultural policy: a case of long-term exclusion', Essex Papers in Politics and Government No. 48, Department of Government, University of Essex.

Smith, M.J. (1990a), 'Pluralism, reformed pluralism and neo-pluralism: the role of pressure groups in policy-making', *Political Studies*, **38** (2), pp. 302–22.

Smith, M.J. (1990b), *The Politics of Agricultural Support in Britain*, Aldershot: Dartmouth.

Smith, M.J. (1991), 'From policy community to issue network: *Salmonella* in eggs and the new politics of food', *Public Administration*, **69** (2), pp. 235–55.

Smith, M.J. (1993), *Pressure, Power and Policy*, Hemel Hempstead: Harvester Wheatsheaf.

Solesbury, W. (1976), 'The environmental agenda', *Public Administration*, 54, pp. 379–97.

Somsen, H. (1994), 'State discretion in European Community environmental law: the case of the Bathing Water Directive', State Autonomy in the European Community research seminar, Christ Church, Oxford.

Spence, D. (1993), 'The role of the national civil service in European lobbying: the British case', in *Lobbying in the European Community*, Mazey, S. and Richardson, J. (eds.), Oxford: Oxford University Press.

Stedward, G. (1987), 'Entry to the system: a case study of women's aid in Scotland', in *Government and Pressure Groups in Britain*, Jordan, A.G. and Richardson, J. (principal authors), Oxford: Clarendon Press.

Stewart, J.D. (1958), *British Pressure Groups*, Oxford: Oxford University Press.

Stitt, S. and Grant, D. (1994), 'Food poverty: Rowntree revisited', in *The Politics of Food*, Henson, S. and Gregory, S. (eds.), Reading: Department of Agricultural Economics and Management, University of Reading.

Stocker, T. (1983), 'Pressures on policy formation', in *The Food Industry: Economics and politics*, Burns, J., McInerney, J. and Swinbank, A. (eds.), London: Heinemann.

Stoker, G. (1991), *The Politics of Local Government*, 2nd edn, London: Macmillan.

Streeck, W. (1983), 'Beyond pluralism and corporatism: German business associations and the state', *Journal of Public Policy*, 3, pp. 265–84.

Streeck, W. and Schmitter, P.C. (1991), 'From national corporatism to transnational pluralism: organized interests in the Single European Market', *Politics and Society*, **19** (2), pp. 133–65.

Stringer, J. and Richardson, J. (1982), 'Policy stability and policy change: industrial training 1964/82', *Public Administration Bulletin*, no. 39, pp. 22–39.

Taylor, E. (1979), *The House of Commons at Work*, 9th edn, London: Macmillan.

Thatcher, M. (1993), *The Downing Street Years*, London: HarperCollins.

Theakston, K. (1987), *Junior Ministers in British Government*, Oxford: Basil Blackwell.

Thomas, R.H. (1983), *The Politics of Hunting*, Aldershot: Gower.

Truman, D. (1951), *The Governmental Process*, New York: Alfred A. Knopf.

Visser, J. and Ebbinghaus, B. (1992), 'Making the most of diversity? European integration and transnational organization of labour', in *Organized Interests in the European Community*, Greenwood, J., Grote, J.R. and Ronit, K. (eds.), London: Sage.

van Waarden, F. (1991), 'Wartime economic mobilisation and state–business relations: a comparison of nine countries', in *Organising Business for War*, Grant, W., Nekkers, J. and van Waarden, F. (eds.), Oxford: Berg.

Walker, J.L. (1991), *Mobilizing Interest Groups in America*, Ann Arbor: University of Michigan Press.

Ward, S. (1993), 'Thinking global, acting local? British local authorities and their environmental plans', *Environmental Politics*, 2 (3), pp. 453–78.

Westergaard, J. and Resler, H. (1976), *Class in a Capitalist Society*, Harmondsworth: Penguin.

Whiteley, P.F. and Winyard, S.J. (1987), *Pressure for the Poor*, London: Methuen.

Wilkinson, P. with Schofield, J. (1994), *Warrior: One man's environmental crusade*, Cambridge: Lutterworth.

Wilson, D. (1984), *Pressure: The A to Z of campaigning in Britain*, London: Heinemann.

Wilson, D. (1988), 'Inside local authorities', *Social Studies Review*, 3 (4), pp. 135–9.

Young, S.C. (1993), *The Politics of the Environment*, Manchester: Baseline.

INDEX

abortion, 76–7, 90
Age Concern, 16
Agriculture, Fisheries and Food,
    Ministry of, 2, 7, 36, 54, 55,
    56, 59, 61, 147, 151
Ainley, P., 38, 39, 156
American Chamber of Commerce,
    115–6
Amery, L., 45
Amnesty International, 32, 81, 137, 138
animal protection movement, 18,
    51, 86, 113, 142, 144
Arp, H.A., 100–1
Association of European
    Automobile Constructors,
    107–8, 116
Atkinson, M.M., 40
Automobile Association, 11, 144

Baldwin, N., 69–70
Barr, G., 143
Beer, S., 39
Berry, S., 83
Blair, T., 157–8
Bose, A., 125
Bown, F., 69
Brickman, R., 90
British Medical Association, 36,
    146, 155

Brittan, A., 40, 41–2, 44
Brooke, R., 95
Browne, W.P., 19, 21
Bruce-Gardyne, J., 57–8, 62, 66, 68,
    70, 72
Buksti, J.A., 139
Burson-Marsteller, 22, 99, 110
business, influence of, 24, 31,
    32–3, 96, 98, 114–8, 161

Cats Protection League, 11
cause groups, 13–14, 32, 66, 85, 89,
    128, 131, 132, 135, 136, 139,
    159, 160, 161, 162
Cawson, A., 109
Chambers, J., 77, 85
charities, 12–13
Chemical Industries Association, 67
Child Poverty Action Group, 87,
    88, 102
Christiansen, L., 19, 139
Church of England, 3, 11–12
Churchill, Sir W., 45
City of London, 4–5, 141, 148
civil service, 57–61, 138–9, 157
Coates, David, 133
Coates, Dudley, 61, 64
Coffin, C., 60
Coleman, W., 40

Committee of Permanent
    Representatives
    (COREPER), 112
Confederation of British Industry
    (CBI), 2, 42, 45, 66–7, 70,
    82–3, 85, 92, 110, 117, 122,
    129, 134, 135, 138, 158–9
Conservative Party, 83, 96, 153, 158
corporatism, 27–8, 37–9, 40, 46,
    121–3, 147–8, 154, 159
Council of Ministers (European),
    100–1, 112–3
Council for the Protection of Rural
    England, 85–6, 91, 93, 144
Cox, G., 37

Danton de Rouffignac, P., 116
Davies, M., 87
democracy, 23–5, 33, 153–4, 159–65
Devlin Commission, 57, 139
Doig, A., 75
Dowding, K., 19, 31, 35, 139
Dowse, R.E., 92
Dudley, G., 58
Dunleavy, P., 15, 29, 30, 136–7, 138

Earth First!, 19
Ebbinghaus, B., 119
Eberlie, R., 122
Eckstein, H., 39
Economic and Social Committee, 114
Edwards, R., 22
Elbaum, B., 43
Elliott, B., 23, 82
Energy, Department of, 58
Environment, Department of, 58, 147
environmental groups, 14–15, 19,
    81, 82, 86, 91, 94–5, 119–20,
    136, 144–5, 161, 162, 164
European Commission, 103, 105–6,
    110–12
European Council of Chemical
    Manufacturing Federations
    (CEFIC), 104–5, 106–7,
    108–9, 113, 116, 119, 120
European Court of Justice, 103, 114
European Parliament, 113
European Round Table, 116–7, 140

European Trade Union
    Confederation, 118–9, 122,
    123

feminism, 5–6
Field, F., 87–8
Finer, S., 39
Franklin, M., 54, 59
Friends of the Earth, 14, 15, 19, 31,
    32, 63, 81, 82, 86, 91, 94–5,
    119, 132, 137, 145

Gardner, J.N., 115, 116
Garner, R., 18, 19, 22, 32, 51, 64,
    78, 86, 120, 142, 144
Germany, 43–4, 107, 132, 147
Gilmour, Lord, 45
Goyder, J., 85, 87, 88, 93
Grant, D., 55
Grantham, C., 71, 74, 75
Green, M.L., 116, 117
Green Alliance, 82
Greenpeace, 15, 19, 22, 81, 82, 86,
    89, 91, 120, 135–6, 137, 138
Greenwood, J., 101, 104, 105, 106,
    109, 112
Grote, J.R., 101, 105, 106, 112

Hall, P., 40
Harvey, B., 133
Heclo, H., 37
Heseltine, M., 45, 132, 134, 147, 156
Hindell, K., 77
Holbeche, B., 57
Hull, R., 105, 110, 111
Hurd, D., 163

implementation of policy, 63–4,
    102–3, 147–9
insider groups, 15, 18, 19–23, 57,
    64–5, 66, 82, 85, 93, 95, 111,
    124, 139, 141, 143, 164
Isaac-Henry, K., 23

Japan, 44, 153
Johansen, L.N., 139
Jordan, G., 6, 8, 10, 14, 16, 19, 20,
    21, 28, 29, 31, 32, 34, 35, 37,

57, 61, 86, 101, 104, 105, 107, 108, 130, 132, 136, 137, 151
Judge, D., 34, 66, 79

King, R., 93
Kingdon, J.W., 50
Kohler-Koch, B., 99, 107, 111, 112, 114

Labour Party, 1, 9, 10, 39, 46, 70, 73, 78, 81, 82–3, 90, 92, 96, 129, 141, 147, 157–9
Lawson, Lord N., 73, 146
Lazonick, W., 43
Liberal Democrats, 46, 96
Lindblom, C.E., 33
Lively, J., 24
local authority associations, 23, 25
London Food Commission, 52–3
Lowe, P., 37, 85, 87, 88, 93
Lynn, L.H., 44

MacDougall, D., 67
McKeown, T.J., 20, 21
McLaughlin, A., 8, 10, 14, 16, 19, 20, 21, 35, 61, 86, 101, 105, 107, 108, 137, 151
McLeay, E.M., 20, 21
Maddox, B., 91
Major, J., 10, 38, 42, 44–5, 146, 157
Malhan, N., 123
Maloney, W., 8, 10, 14, 16, 19, 20, 21, 35, 61, 86, 91, 101, 105, 108, 137, 151
Marsh, D., 29, 35, 76, 77, 85, 90
Martinelli, A., 109
May, T., 20
Mazey, S., 99, 101, 102, 104, 105, 112, 113, 114, 116, 117, 120, 121, 124
Medhurst, K., 12
media, 49, 50, 52, 53–4, 56, 84–9
Miller, C., 60, 63, 65, 68, 73
Miller, D., 54
Mills, M., 56
Mitchell, J., 121
Mitchell, N.J., 145
Moe, T., 32

Moran, M., 138
Moravcsik, A., 117
Motor Cycle Action Group, 17–18, 21, 121
Moyser, G., 12

National Economic Development Council, 38
National Farmers' Union, 2, 9, 20, 36, 57, 67, 72, 94, 125, 133–4, 136, 150–2, 158–9
National Federation of Old Age Pensioners' Associations, 16, 19
National Federation of Retirement Pensions Associations, 16, 17
National Food Alliance, 53, 54
Nekkers, J., 44
Nettl, J.P., 22–3
Newby, H., 94
Newton, K., 92
Norton, P., 63, 69
Nugent, N., 20

Offe, C., 33
Olson, M., 30–31, 32–3, 42–4, 161
outsider groups, 15, 18, 19–23, 55, 95, 119, 121, 142–3

Paterson, W., 44, 58
Plowden, W., 58, 158
pluralism, 28–34
policy communities, 34–7, 154, 164
policy networks, 34, 154
political parties, 8–9, 34, 67, 80–3, 153–4, 164
Porritt, J., 81, 86, 88, 89, 147, 161
Pratt, H.J., 16, 17, 133
Presthus, R., 28, 130, 131–2

quasi-governmental organisations, 7–8

Ramblers' Association, 15, 142
Read, M., 76, 77, 90
Reilly, J., 74
Resler, H., 34
Rhodes, R.A.W., 25, 35

Richardson, J.J., 6, 14, 29, 34, 37, 42,
    57, 91, 99, 101, 102, 104, 112,
    113, 114, 116, 117, 120, 124
Riddell, P., 72
Robinson, M., 81–2, 93, 145, 148
Ronit, K., 101, 106, 109, 112
Rose, R., 143–4
Royal Society for the Protection of
    Animals (RSPCA), 19, 32,
    51, 64
Royal Society for the Protection of
    Birds (RSPB), 1, 10–11, 15,
    120, 137
Rucht, D., 89, 114, 119–20, 136
Rüdig, W., 91
Rush, M., 71, 72

Salisbury, R.H., 25, 121
Sandholtz, W., 117
Sargent, J., 102
Schattschneider, E.E., 33
Schmitter, P.C., 114, 118, 121, 123,
    124, 130, 131, 134
Scottish Nationalists, 67
sectional groups, 2, 13–14, 32, 66,
    67, 70–1, 74, 89, 128, 131,
    135, 136, 139, 159, 163–4
Self, P., 9
Seyd, P., 82, 92
Seymour-Ure, C., 71, 74, 75
Simms, M., 77
Smith, M., 28, 33, 50, 55, 118, 125,
    133–4, 146, 150, 151
social movements, 5–6
Society of Teachers Opposed to
    Physical Punishment
    (STOPP), 149
Solesbury, W., 50
Somsen, H., 103
Spence, D., 101, 103, 112
Stedward, G., 6
Stewart, J.D., 13–14
Stitt, S., 55
Stocker, T., 59
Stoker, G., 95, 96
Storing, H.J., 9
Streeck, W., 114, 118, 121, 123,
    124, 130, 131, 132, 134
Stringer, J., 37

Taylor, E., 63, 76
Thatcher Government, 12, 42, 49,
    78–9, 148
Thatcherism, 10, 38, 40–1, 42, 43,
    70, 146, 155–7
Theakston, K., 59–60, 61, 62
think tanks, 9–10
Thomas, R.H., 78
Trade and Industry, Department
    of, 7, 58, 147, 157
trade unions, 38, 39, 41, 95, 96,
    118–9, 122, 138, 140–1, 145,
    156, 159
Trades Union Congress, 42, 145–6
Transport, Department of, 58, 147
Truman, D., 29, 31

Union of Industrial and Employers'
    Confederations of Europe
    (UNICE), 115, 122, 123

Vickerstaff, S., 38, 39, 156
Visser, J., 119

van Waarden, F., 44
Waldegrave, W., 146–7
Walker, J.L., 31, 32, 33, 52, 53
Ward, S., 94
Westergaard, J., 34
Whiteley, P., 16, 58, 60–1, 62, 81,
    88, 89, 90, 92, 127, 129, 131,
    132, 135, 141, 146
Whitston, C., 44, 58
Wiesenthal, H., 33
Wildavsky, A., 37
Wilkinson, P., 140
Wilson, David, 96
Wilson, Des, 159–63
Winner, D., 81, 86, 88, 89, 147, 161
Winter, M., 37
Winyard, S., 16, 58, 60–1, 62, 88,
    89, 90, 127, 129, 130, 131,
    132, 135, 141, 146
World Wide Fund for Nature, 15,
    19, 138, 145

Young, S.C., 162

Zysman, J., 117